MAGAZINE

POCKET GUIDE TO
SPIRITS

Everything You Need to Know
to Buy and Enjoy Spirits

RUNNING PRESS
PHILADELPHIA · LONDON

9   8   7   6   5   4   3   2   1

Digit on the right indicates the number of this printing

Library of Congress Control Number: 2008926179

ISBN 978-0-7624-3187-8

Cover and interior design by Corinda Cook
Edited by Kristen Green Wiewora
Special thanks to Martha Hopkins
Photo research by Susan Oyama
Typography: Avenir, Caslon, and Univers

Running Press Book Publishers
2300 Chestnut Street
Philadelphia, PA 19103-4371

Visit us on the web!
www.runningpress.com

Contents

Distilled Spirits in the Third Millennium

Tray of various cocktails

In the first decade of the third millennium, distilled spirits are sizzling in the marketplace. Distilled spirits include whiskeys (such as Scotch, Bourbon, Tennessee sour mash, Canadian, Irish, Japanese, and North American blended), brandies (like Cognac, Armagnac, Calvados, pisco, *eaux-de-vie*, marc, and grappa), liqueurs, and white spirits (such as vodka, gin, mescal, Tequila, rum, and cachaça). In the view of many industry observers, spirits have never been more in style on a global basis than they are right now.

Spirits sales in the U.S. market rose by a healthy 7.5 percent in 2005 and by 6.3 percent in 2006, according to statistics provided by the Washington, D.C.-based Distilled Spirits Council of the United States (DISCUS). The areas of the most vigorous growth were in premium and super-premium sectors. In both of those years, distilled spirits captured a larger share of total beverage alcohol sales among beer, wine, and spirits. Currently, there are more spirits brands available to U.S. consumers than ever before.

Why are spirits so white-hot? There are four reasons, a sort of "perfect storm" of compelling marketplace forces that ultimately drive an entire beverage alcohol category.

First and foremost is the growing sophistication of the collective global consumer palate over the past quarter century. Since the 1970s, when the post-World War II era of processed food and bland eating faded and was forcibly replaced by the new age of authentic cooking and fine dining, the average consumer has leapt forward in both culinary and beverage experience and knowledge.

Following the lead of the now-legendary chefs who so improved our eating habits like James Beard, Julia Child, Alice Waters, Wolfgang Puck, Larry Forgione, and Andre Soltner, consumers also became interested in what they were drinking as well as eating. That interest gave birth to the wine boom of the 1980s. Further sophistication spawned the craft-brewing explosion of the 1990s. Fine spirits were the next logical segment for savvy consumers to investigate.

The expansion of international trade made this feasible. Attractive trade tariffs and multinational trade agreements over the last twenty to thirty years have meant that more products from more nations are available in increasing numbers of markets. Most of the top spirits categories, like Scotch whisky, Cognac, vodka, and gin, are available in more than 200 nations.

With the increasingly sophisticated palate of consumers and easy trade of spirits worldwide, distillers have answered the call for better and better products. As consumer interest has exploded, distillers have brought out their best spirits to keep pace with the competition. This has created a Garden of Eden for the world's consumers, wherein the variety and scope of spirits have leapt forward.

When you add in the indefatigable consumer fascination with cocktails, you have the fourth component of this perfect storm. The public's interest in mixed drinks has grown significantly, both within the home and in restaurants and bars. As creative mixologists have broadened the definitions of many of the classic cocktails, the demand for better spirits has risen in direct proportion. The theme of "better ingredients make better cocktails" has been the driving force behind the dramatic growth of both mixed drinks and fine spirits as consumers are willing to pay for a more authentic and pleasurable imbibing experience.

Raise your glasses to the new golden age of spirits.

Spirits can find a place in all types of celebrations.

CHAPTER ONE

Water of Life

A martini glass with olive

The pedigree of distilled beverages

Latin-speaking medieval Christian monks called them *aqua vitae*. The monks' contemporaries in France referred to them as *eaux-de-vie*. Gaelic-speaking distillers in Ireland and Scotland identified them as *uisge beatha*. Poles and Russians labeled them as *zhizennia voda*. All of these mellifluous monikers meant one thing: *water of life*.

These names referred to the fermented and distilled liquids that by the fifteenth century had become firmly rooted in societies from Russia, Poland, Scandinavia, Germany, and the British Isles in Europe's northern tier to France, Spain, Italy, and Greece in the south. But what was meant by *water of life*? The meaning has to do with how distilled liquids were viewed and how they were used for centuries as restoratives and medicines.

Spirits come about through two necessary transformative processes: fermentation and distillation. Well prior to the discovery of the process of distillation, which most likely occurred in or around the region of what is today Pakistan and northern India, Eurasian farmers utilized fermentation to convert commonplace fruit juices, especially grape juice, and grain mashes into low-alcohol (5 to 12 percent) beverages. With fermentation, alcohol, carbon dioxide, and heat are generated when yeast—a universally available microorganism—consumes innate sugars in either fruit juices or mashes of grain.

This natural biochemical process is triggered whenever sugary liquids come into contact with either airborne or purposely injected yeasts. Because fruit juices are innately sugary, wines can—under the right circumstances—virtually make themselves. But a bit of human intervention always helps, particularly with flavor.

When did fermentation and distillation begin?

Fermented beverages very likely existed before historical events were formally recorded. Early agrarian communities from 3000 B.C.E. and before have displayed indisputable archeological evidence of winemaking and brewing. Pinpointing exactly when fermentation took flight within the framework of an ancient community must be left to speculation.

Regarding distillation, however, historians now have a relatively clear sense of when this second step may have first bubbled to the surface. Archeological digs conducted in the 1960s in the ancient Greek-Indian city of Shaikhan Dheri in Pakistan unearthed compelling evidence of earthen pot stills that suggested the existence of small-scale distilleries. Similar findings near modern-day Peshawar, a city in northern Pakistan located near the Khyber Pass, have appeared in various reports. Adding to the discovery are textural interpretations in India's Vedic literature that appear to support the archeological discoveries of the twentieth century, drawing tantalizing attention to the period of around 500 C.E. as a possible launching date for distillation, though it would not reach Europe for another 500 years.

In the last quarter of the eighth century C.E., Abu

Musa Jabir Ibn Haiyan of Kufa (present-day Iraq) invented a pot still fashioned out of copper known as the alembic still. Ibn Haiyan realized that earthen or ceramic pot stills were neither as efficient nor reliable conductors of heat as malleable metals, most specifically, copper. What Jabir Ibn Haiyan created was nothing less than the modern, onion-shaped copper kettle that is still in use today around the entire world.

Two centuries later in Persia (today's Iran), Abu Ali al-Husain Ibn Abdullah Ibn Sina, a noted physician, educator, and author of 450 books and essays, catapulted Ibn Haiyan's distillation methods further by extensively writing about the vital importance of gathering, cooling, and condensing the alcoholic vapors to create the quintessence of the process, the pure spirit. Abdullah Ibn Sina, referred to in Europe as Avicenna, used his prominence within Middle Eastern culture to establish distillation in the Arabic sciences.

Little wonder, then, that the words alcohol and alembic are derived from Arabic terms. *Al-koh'l* is Arabic for "antimony powder," the powder utilized as a base for cosmetics, and *al-'anbik* translates to "the still."

Three centuries after the invasion of Europe's Iberian Peninsula by the Islamic Moors in the eighth century C.E., the instruction of distillation turned up in the Salerno School of Medicine in Italy. The Benedictine Order operated the school, producing educated missionaries, physicians, and clergy. Over the subsequent two to three centuries, distillation spread throughout western Europe along with the opening of Christian monasteries, hospitals, and abbeys.

A Carthusian monk in the distillery at the Monastery of the Grande Chartreuse in Dauphine, southeastern France, makes the famous Chartreuse liqueur from a blend of 130 herbs.

Over time, the monks became highly skilled distillers, and they routinely dispensed their soothing and restorative homemade spirits packed with herbs, spices, and honey to weary travelers and the infirm or dying.

Influential doctors of the period, most notably Arnaldus de Villa Nova, the thirteenth-century physician to popes and kings, advanced the cause of distillation even further through their espousal of the method. Their water of life elixirs gained popularity with Europe's aristocracy. Soon, other schools of medicine like those at Avignon and Montpellier, France, taught the art of distillation.

The period between 1000 C.E. and 1300 C.E. proved to be the dawn of the first great age of distilled spirits. By the mid-sixteenth century, Europe's noble class used their influence and riches to transform distillation and distilled spirits from a rustic abbey cellar hobby into an increasingly sophisticated minor industry.

Ancient Uses of Distillation

Interestingly, the ancient civilizations that became proficient in distilling didn't use it for the making of recreational libations as we do today. It wasn't until distillation became widespread in Europe in the fourteenth century C.E. that spirits were consumed for pleasure as much as for medicinal reasons or to salve over the everyday horrors of medieval life.

Indian physicians in the first millennium created medicines through distillation that were administered for topical and internal ailments. Dynastic Chinese distillers boiled fermented liquids to make potions that purportedly enhanced sexuality, encouraged youthful behavior, and reversed aging. Priests in Pharaonic Egypt used distillation to make their god-like royalty exotic perfumes out of flower oils and effective cosmetics that would hold up in the blazing desert sun. Alchemists in ancient Greece employed distillation in their futile pursuit of turning ordinary, non-precious metals into gold.

What is distillation?

In the ominously titled *Das Buch zu Destilliern*, sixteenth-century German author Hieronymous Braunschweig defined distillation as "Distylling is none other thynge, but onely a puryfyeng of the grosse from the subtyll and the subtyll from the grosse."

The subtyll from the grosse. Those five words tidily sum up distillation better than any long-winded description.

The word distillation is derived from *destillare*, the Latin verb meaning "to drip down." At its most fundamental, distillation is a purification process that utilizes concentrated heat to boil fermented liquids, such as beer and wine, for the express purpose of separating the alcohol from the water and base materials. Alcohol boils at precisely 173.1 degrees Fahrenheit, while water boils at 212 degrees Fahrenheit, so the alcohol turns gaseous before the water turns to steam.

This procedure works best when carried out in a kettle or any variety of mechanical contraptions, where intense heat can be generated and sustained and in which vapors can be captured. These kettles are referred to as "pot stills." As the alcohol changes from liquid into vapor, it rises in the pot still's chambers and is guided through channels whereupon it cools and condenses, dripping back down into clear liquid form. The intense heat of distillation strips away impurities in fermented liquids, preserving only the liquid's essence. With each round of distillation, the liquid contains fewer contaminants and the percentage of alcohol increases.

Pot Stills and Column Stills

For approximately twenty-three centuries, there was but a solitary way to distill liquids: the pot still method. For the last thirteen hundred years, the pot-bellied, kettle-like pot still has been made of metal, predominantly copper. Copper has been preferred because it is strong, yet more malleable than other metals.

The concept of pot still distillation is direct in its simplicity. Here's how it works, step-by-step:

• The distiller pumps fermented liquid (beer or wine) into the chamber of the pot still.

- The pot still is heated, gradually bringing the alcohol to the boil, whereupon it vaporizes.

- The vapors ascend into the upper region of the pot still chamber and flow through a swan neck pipe at the top of the pot still.

- The vapors move from the swan neck through to cooled coils where they condense, turning back into liquid form (spirits), purer, clearer, and higher in alcohol than when they started.

Copper whisky stills at a distillery in Scotland

• The distiller carefully captures the middle part of the distillation run, the best portion or so-called "heart" (similar to the best cuts of meats, like the center cuts, tenderloins, or filets) and separates that prime segment from the rest of the run.

• The less pure parts of the distillation run, the "heads" and "tails" are often put through another distillation to purify them to the desired degree.

• Many single-batch spirits are distilled again in other smaller pot stills to elevate levels of purity and alcohol yet further.

The resultant spirits are typically high in quality and distinctive in character. Fresh, virgin spirits right off a pot still have a floral or fruity fragrance and are also crystal clear in appearance. Once this basic sequence of individual batch distilling is completed, the pot still requires cleaning before the next batch of fermented liquid can be placed into the pot still chamber.

This age-old method, while expensive and labor-intensive, remains a reliable source for thousands of the world's finest distilled spirits. But even though it's the *original* way of distilling liquids, the pot still individual batch method isn't the *only* way to produce quality spirits.

Column Distillation

Beginning in the first decades of the Industrial Revolution, a Scottish distiller named Robert Stein introduced an innovative, more efficient, and less expensive process. Stein, who made spirits at the Kilbagie Distillery in Clackmannanshire, devised the first patented model of the single-column method in 1827. His metal columnar still ran continuously and didn't need to be stopped and cleaned.

Shortly thereafter, another inventor-distiller, Irishman Aeneas Coffey, took Stein's design and added even more height to the cylindrical column, thereby increasing the purity of the distillate as well as the volume of the output.

Here's how Coffey's revolutionary still design worked: The base of the column was called the analyzer and the top tier was known as the rectifier. Every section enclosed a series of chambers that were separated by perforated metal plates. As alcohol vapors rose through each plate, more impurities collided with the plates and fell back down the chamber, allowing purer vapors to advance up the chamber. Coffey discovered that the taller the column, the cleaner the resultant spirit.

Other distillers added another column to Coffey's basic design and were soon making ethereal spirits of remarkable purity, quality, and lightness with a double-column system. Soon, this still was being referred to as the patent still, Coffey still, or column still.

What was obvious to the distilling industry across the world by the 1870s was that this new, efficient, industrial, low-cost, continuously functioning process—and the precise opposite of customary, stop-and-start, labor-intensive pot still distillation—was the wave of the future for creating large volumes of spirits. Nowadays, the process called "continuous distillation" is practiced in every nation that produces spirits and is the distillation of choice for the majority of lighter, mostly unaged spirits like rum, gin, vodka, and cachaça.

Many distillers use both pot distillation and column distillation, frequently in tandem, to produce high-grade

Copper pot stills of the Glenlivet whisky distillery in Scotland

spirits that contain elements of each system. Pot stills preserve the character of the initial ingredients, while column stills result in purer, cleaner, high-content alcohols.

A prime example of a world-class spirit with international acceptance is blended Scotch whisky. Master blenders from renowned companies, such as Chivas Brothers, Dewar's, Ballantine's, Berry Brothers, and Johnnie Walker, marry multiple whiskies from column stills made in large industrial complexes and single malt whiskies made in pot stills at smaller distilleries to create a highly palatable blend of the two styles.

Beyond fermentation and distillation, aging and storage can have a marked effect on a spirit's flavor. Some distillates are stored in wood barrels.

How wood maturation affects spirits

Why are some distillates placed in wood barrels? Why are wood barrels employed in the maturation process rather than some other form of vessel?

The concept of using wooden barrels for storage and the shipping of wares hit stride with the Romans by the third century. Clay *amphorae,* ceramic vessels with long, narrow necks, were widely used for transport in the Mediterranean region since the time of the Phoenicians and the Greeks, but clay pots cracked and broke too easily. By the end of the second century, Roman commercial shippers and merchants began replacing their amphorae with wood barrels that could be easily rolled and stacked onto ships. They constructed barrels out of palm wood in order to transport common goods, like olive oil, olives, dried fruit, wine, nails, dried herbs, and gold coins, across the Roman Empire via ocean-going vessels.

Wood barrels had one more virtue that shippers liked: in the event of a shipwreck, wood barrels floated. Amphorae sank like rocks. So, for durability, ease of movement, stacking, and recovery, wood barrels became indispensable.

What European merchants found in the ensuing centuries was that wine and spirits changed for the better when stored in wood barrels. They mellowed, darkened, and became far more drinkable due to the influence of acids found in wood, in particular lignin and tannin.

Wood also allowed the encased liquid to breathe. The moderate contact with air softened the spirits, making them more drinkable. Over the centuries, winemakers and distillers moved to oak because they found that it has the ideal level of porosity that lets spirits and wines mature gradually and evenly.

As the skill of cooperage (barrel-making) became more advanced by the nineteenth century, spirits merchants came to the conclusion that certain types of oak imparted very specific qualities to the spirits. For instance, American oak, which is aggressive in its youth, affects a whiskey or a brandy with subtle flavors sometimes akin to coconut, tropical fruit (banana, especially), chocolate, clove, sawdust, or butterscotch. French oak, on the other hand, can give off spicier, zestier notes, possibly of ginger, vanilla, black pepper, allspice, toffee, or nutmeg.

Cognac from the Borderies area aging in barrel in one of the many warehouses of Courvoisier

Proper barrel selection for whiskey, brandy, Tequila, and rum has become an auxiliary industry of its own. Choosing the right barrel type can greatly affect spirits' values at the termination of the aging period. Some single-malt whisky distillers in Scotland make the argument that oak barrels influence the ultimate taste profile of a whisky by as much as 60 to 80 percent.

Distillers of American straight Bourbon whiskeys (whiskeys that contain a minimum of 51 percent corn) can legally only use their oak barrels once in the aging of their whiskeys. Cognac and Armagnac distillers in France prefer to buy new barrels for the aging of their fine brandies.

Some spirits categories routinely buy oak barrels that had been used to store other types of alcoholic beverages. Prime examples include the Scots who as a matter of course purchase thousands of barrels each year from America's Bourbon industry (who by law can use them for maturation but once) as well as from Spain's Sherry producers. The same holds true for rum and Tequila producers.

The bottom line is that every admirer of spirits should know that wood maturation plays an enormous part in the fashioning of whiskeys, brandies, and some Tequilas, liqueurs, and rums.

CHAPTER TWO

White Spirits:
Vodka, Gin, Mescal, Tequila, Rum, and Cachaça

The gin and tonic with lime is one of the most popular mixed gin drinks around.

What are white spirits?

The categorical name "white spirits" is somewhat deceiving. What causes much of the confusion for consumers is that the majority of the so-called white spirits are, in fact, clear as rainwater with no pigmentation whatsoever. Yet some older rums and Tequilas sport coloring from pale straw to deep brown, born from the influence of oak barrels (Tequila) or simple and legal cosmetic coloring (rum) or sometimes both (rum).

Gin and vodka are related, if for no other reason than they are the "clearest" of the white spirits. Tequila and mescal, both from Mexico, share a common bond in that they both are produced from different strains of the same botanical genus of agave. Rum, made from sugar refining by-products, and cachaça, Brazil's sugarcane-based spirit, are second cousins. While they will all be grouped under the umbrella of white spirits, there are marvelous similarities and differences that distinguish them all.

VODKA

History of Vodka

The word vodka is derived from the Russian and Polish *zhizenennia voda*, which translates, like aqua vitae, to "water of life." Though evidence is unclear, some historians believe that a primitive form of vodka was sporadically available throughout what are now Poland, Ukraine, and Russia as early as the thirteenth and fourteenth centuries and throughout Scandinavia by the late fourteenth century.

Early vodkas were created out of any variety of crops that could be cultivated above or below ground in the cold, harsh climate of northern and eastern Europe, such as potatoes, beets, and grains like wheat, rye, oats, and barley. Most vodkas produced in the Middle Ages were primitive beverages that were flavored with honey, herbs, and spices to make them more palatable. Their alcohol content was likely no more than 25 percent, due to the crude and inefficient pot stills of the period.

Vodka, the global phenomenon

Gin, Bourbon, blended American whiskey, and Scotch whisky were the spirits of choice from the end of Prohibition in 1933 through the mid 1960s. In the 1950s, the producers of made-in-Connecticut, Russian-sounding Smirnoff Vodka started an aggressive advertising and marketing campaign that used celebrities and the phrase "Smirnoff leaves you breathless," implying that as opposed to other popular spirits—like brandy, gin, and

Vodka martinis are made by shaking vodka and vermouth together with ice cubes before straining into a cocktail glass. Any number of flavorings can be added.

whiskey—vodka didn't leave the scent of alcohol on one's breath.

Heublein, Smirnoff's parent company, also pushed vodka as a key and revolutionary cocktail ingredient in mixed drinks such as the Moscow mule, screwdriver, vodka gimlet, and vodkatini. Vodka continues to be a highly favored base ingredient for cocktails today, though it should be pointed out that gin is making marginal gains with many influential mixologists in pivotal metropolitan areas.

In 1967, vodka passed gin in case sales in the U.S. marketplace for the first time in history. In 1976, vodka overtook North American blended whiskey (Seagram's VO and Seagram's 7 Crown, in particular, which had held the number one and two spots for decades) and became the leading spirits segment in categorical sales.

Worldwide, vodka sales now account for one out of every four bottles of distilled spirits sold. Vodka is wildly popular worldwide for two reasons: From a distiller's perspective, it can be made anywhere from virtually anything for not a great deal of money and, if marketed right, can return substantial margins on investment.

From a mixologist's perspective, no other spirit mixes as well in a wide array of cocktails as vodka. Since vodka's attributes are so subtle, it complements scores of cocktail ingredients. More cocktails have vodka as their base spirit than any other type of distillate. In short, the sheer numbers of production volume, net revenues earned, and possible applications of the product are on the side of vodka more than any other category of distillate.

So what, exactly, is vodka?

The overwhelming majority of vodkas are fermented and distilled neutral grain spirits, or ethyl alcohol. Definitions of vodka, when they exist at all, unfortunately add to the confusion about it. The U.S. government, for example, carelessly defines vodka as being ". . . without distinctive character, aroma, taste, or color . . ." yet many premium and super-premium vodkas are, in fact, highly individual, flavorful, and distinctive.

Any vodka's character is generated mainly from two sources: the base material and the material used in the filtering process. Choosing the particular base material for vodka production depends on the preference of the distiller and also the tradition of the locale and distillery.

The majority of modern vodkas are produced from grains, such as wheat, rye, corn, or barley, and grasses, specifically, sugar cane. These vodkas tend to be light, smooth, and as neutral as vodka gets. Some vodkas are produced from potatoes, especially in Poland and in Idaho and Maine. Potato vodkas are typically heavier in texture and sweeter in taste than those made from grain. Vodkas produced from fruits, like apples or grapes, are tart and mildly fruity. In the last half decade, a minor movement has taken hold, both in Europe and the U.S., in using wine grapes as a base material. In Vermont, one distiller even employs maple syrup as a foundation. Others have used beetroot, pumpkins, carrots, and onions.

Because vodka is produced all around the globe from many different substances, there are no hard and fast rules governing it that apply in the same way that, say, Scotch whisky (made only in Scotland), Bourbon (produced only in the U.S.), Cognac (distilled only in France) or Tequila (made solely in Mexico) operate under strict regulations. That is not to imply that vodka is inferior to other more tightly controlled spirits. Due to the unwieldy logistics of a spirit made from any assortment of ingredients, it simply isn't as closely regulated.

Then, of course, there are the flavored vodkas. People have been adding flavorings since the Middle Ages, primarily to mask the deficiencies of early distillation. The most typical flavors come from fruit essences, namely, lemon, lime, orange, raspberry, strawberry, peach, black currant, pineapple, tangerine, pear, and cranberry. Other contemporary flavorings include vanilla, coffee, cinnamon, chile pepper, grass, and chocolate. Most are every bit as high in quality as their unflavored siblings.

How vodkas are filtered also affects their character. Charcoal filtering, the most prevalent, imparts a hint of sweet smokiness, almost a sooty quality. Quartz crystals lend a stony, mineral-like kind of taste, while cloth or fiber panel filtering gives off an aroma of parchment or cotton fabric.

How is vodka made?

Vodka requires only three ingredients: water, yeast, and the grain or other base material of choice. The ingredients are combined into a soupy mash and then fermented into a low-alcohol liquid, normally between 6 and 11 percent alcohol. The fermented mash is then distilled most often in continuously running column stills until the alcohol level reaches 96.4 percent, whereupon it is considered a neutral grain spirit (ethyl alcohol).

Currently, only a smattering of premium and super-premium vodkas are distilled in the traditional batch process in small, labor-intensive copper pot stills. Column stills offer greater efficiency and volume, yielding a cleaner, purer high-alcohol spirit that can be quickly filtered, bottled, and placed in the commercial current of the marketplace within weeks.

With some exceptions in eastern Europe, vodka is not aged in wood barrels. Wood maturation or aging of any kind, in fact, undercuts the premise of vodka, which is as a fresh, clean, unaged spirit. With no time wasted on wood maturation or long storage in warehouses, vodkas are reliable moneymakers for distillers.

GIN

The history of gin

The name comes from the French term for juniper, *genièvre*. Legend has for decades erroneously claimed that Holland was the birthplace of gin and that a Dutch doctor named Franciscus de la Boe created it as a remedy for kidney problems around 1650. De la Boe was, in actuality, a prominent proponent of gin, but not its inventor.

The myth about de la Boe as gin's creator has been debunked by the discovery of writings from thirteenth-century France in which juniper was employed as an additive to *aqua vitae* by the most illustrious physician of the late Middle Ages, Arnaud de Villa Nova, a doctor to kings, royalty, and popes.

Other vague reports claim that juniper-laced libations existed in England and the low countries of

Gin and tonic with lime

Belgium and Holland in the late 1500s. For the moment, it's best to conclude that the origins of gin deserve further debate and more scholarly investigation. The birth of gin was likely to have occurred between the fourteenth and sixteenth centuries, somewhere in the region that comprises modern-day northern France, Holland, and Belgium.

During the nineteenth century, concoctions such as gin punch (England) and the India tonic (India) gained popularity throughout the British Empire. In North America, gin slings and the gin cocktail were widely known in the early 1800s. Gin's status was cemented as a must-have spirit when some bright spark mixed it with vermouth, creating the indispensable dry martini. Today, gin is considered to be among the classiest of all spirits categories and is looked upon as a supremely worthy ingredient to a host of new and classic cocktails.

What is gin?

Gin is, in the widest sense, a grain-based vodka flavored with juniper berries. There are 60 to 70 species of the aromatic evergreen trees or shrubs of the *Juniperus* genus of the cypress family, and the fragrant, cedary-piney smelling berries are frequently used in the flavoring of gin.

Though juniper is first among gin flavorings, there exists an astounding menu of other compounds used in gin. Other key botanicals, which distillers may or may not use, include roots such as angelica, orris, and ginger; herbs and pods like coriander, caraway, aniseed, rosemary, and cardamom; dried fruit peels like orange, lime, tangerine, and lemon; barks such as cassia; spices, most notably, cumin, and nutmeg; plants and flowers like fennel, licorice, cucumber, and rose petals; nuts like almonds; and non-juniper berries such as cubeb berries and grains of paradise.

In order to achieve the desired house style, each distiller employs his or her own closely guarded recipe of botanical ratios every time. Some distillers infuse the oils of botanicals into their neutral grain spirits while others steep mixtures of whole, fresh botanicals into them during a second stage of distillation.

On all accounts, distillation is the production phase where botanicals are introduced. The key lies in making certain that the properties that you want are accented and the ones you want muted remain in the background supporting roles. Angelica root, for example, is a botanical that is employed more as a unifying factor than as a flavoring agent on its own. Because of the delicate balance of the botanicals, gin is an extremely difficult spirit to produce in a consistent style.

Juniper berries, with their cedar-pine scent, are the basis of the flavor in gin.

Styles of gin

- **Genever.** Genevers are the traditional style of perfumed and deeply flavorful gins that are made in the Netherlands, and they are as close to the original style of gin as one can achieve at present. There are three categories: *junge* (young), *oude* (matured), and flavored. Genevers are the only gins that are aged in wood barrels, and they differ dramatically from the satiny-smooth London dry gins in that they are more pungent, textured, and prickly. Most Genevers remain in Holland for consumption, but it's of little consequence to the U.S. consumers, who prefer the dry variety with a lighter, more aromatic, and more mixable style.

- **Old Tom.** Old Tom was a thick, sweetened style of gin that appealed to the masses of eighteenth-century London and was, in large measure, the sickly elixir that caused an epidemic of drunkenness across Great Britain in the first half of the 1700s. Old Tom eventually gave rise to the creation of London dry gin, a cleaner, crisper type that remains the sophisticated world's favorite variety of gin to this day.

- **London dry.** When you see the words "London dry gin" on the label, they signify only the dry, lighter style of gin, not the city of production. Indeed, only Beefeater London dry gin is produced in London. London dry gins focus more on the juniper presence than do Genevers and, thus, are better cocktail gins.

The founders of the London dry styles include James Burroughs (Beefeater, 1863); the Booth Family (Booth's, 1770s); Sir Robert Burnett (Burnett's White Satin, 1770);

Walter and Alfred Gilbey (Gilbey's, 1857); Alexander Gordon (Gordon's, 1769); G & J Greenall (Greenall's, 1761); and Charles Tanqueray (Tanqueray, 1830).

• **Plymouth gin.** The Coates family and their Black-friars Distillery on England's southwest coast are credited with creating the Plymouth gin in 1793. Plymouth gin has a style of its own. Whereas the more prevalent London dry style plays up the cedary-Christmas tree juniper flavoring, Plymouth is accentuated by other botanicals, especially orris and angelica roots as well as citrus peels like lemon and orange. The result is one of the finest gins in the marketplace.

Mescal and Tequila

All agave-based spirits of Mexico, including mescal and Tequila, are collected beneath the over-arching categorical name of mescal. So mescal, then, is both a spirits category associated solely with Mexico and a particular subcategory of agave spirits made in and around Oaxaca, Mexico, within that category.

Tequila is a subcategory of mescal in a similar way that Scotch whisky or Bourbon are subcategories of the greater whiskey category, or Cognac and Armagnac are subcategories of the brandy category. While there are several regional styles of Mexican agave-based spirits distilled (Sotol, Bacanora, and Comiteca among them), Tequila and mescal are, by far, the most prominent on the international stage.

Mescal, Tequila, and other agave-based spirits are created in Mexico from the fermented and distilled juice of agave plants. Much to the surprise of most Tequila lovers, the agave plant is not a cactus; rather, it is but one of a family of succulents from the lily family with hundreds of defined species under the botanical name *agavacea*.

Farmers who cultivate agaves over tens of thousands of acres throughout west-central and southern Mexico collectively prefer the customary agricultural name, *maguey*, to agave. The term *maguey*, pronounced "mah-gay," is derived from the Náhuatl Indian word, *mahayuel* ("ma-ha-hwell"), an ancient term that was employed centuries ago when native Aztec holy men invoked the god of the plant.

Like any other type of botanical genus, the agave family tree includes many distinct strains. Some botanists now estimate that there may be as many as 400 individual types of agave. American gardeners are familiar with ornamental agaves, especially yucca and century plants that thrive in warm, dry climates and poor soils. Other types of agave are grown throughout the tropics not for their juice, but for their leaf fibers which, when processed, make strong grades of cords, like sisal hemp.

It generally takes a minimum of five to six years for an agave plant to grow ready for harvest. From the farmers' standpoint, agave farming is a long-term enterprise and investment.

The part of the agave that is essential is the pineapple-like *piña*, or heart. Mature piñas can weigh anywhere from 60 to 100 pounds. Some of the largest weigh in at 115 to 125 pounds. Workers, called *jimadors*, trim the piñas of their spikes right in the field. To make a spirit from agave piñas, the piñas must first be both cooked and shredded, then the juice is milled from the materials.

History of agave-based drinks

With regard to agave-based beverages, the first such liquid in pre-Colombian Mexico was *pulque* (pronounced puhl-kay). Aztec farmers cultivated agave plants and made this naturally fermented, milky-looking drink from sweet, syrupy agave juice. Pulque has a low five- to seven- percent alcohol. A common misconception is that modern-day Tequila and mescal are created out of pulque. That is incorrect. Each is distilled from fermented agave juice, which bears little resemblance to traditional pulque.

Following the Conquistador invasion in 1519, Spanish settlers introduced pot still distillation to Mexico. (Some sketchy evidence has recently come to light, which points to the possibility that distillation in Mexico preceded the Conquistadors.) Whatever the case, we have evidence of agave-based distillates soon after the Spanish arrived and conquered Mexico. These raw, crude spirits were the progenitors of Tequila and mescal.

Juice of the blue agave plant, like the one above, is fermented and twice-distilled to make 100-percent agave Tequila.

Tequila

All Tequila is produced in five west-central Mexican states of Jalisco, Nayarit, Michoacán, Guanajuato, and Tamaulipas. Jalisco is the epicenter of the Tequila industry and is home to the town of Tequila as well as most of the distilleries.

Tequila is legally made in two fundamental types: 100-percent agave and mixto. Those bottled as "100-percent agave" are comprised totally from the fermented and twice-distilled juice of the blue agave plant. The official botanical moniker of blue agave is *Agave tequiliana weber azul*, named after the German botanist, F. Weber, who classified agaves at the turn of the twentieth century.

Straight Tequila is sometimes drunk as a shooter by licking a pinch of salt, taking a Tequila shot, and then sucking on a wedge of lemon or lime.

The lesser class of Tequila, *mixto* (pronounced "mees-toe") is a marriage of convenience between pure blue agave spirits and sugar cane-based spirits. The saving grace of mixtos is that, by law, blue agave distillate makes up the majority (51 percent) of the blend.

To produce Tequila, agave piñas are usually steamed in large, cylindrical, stainless-steel steamers called autoclaves. High-quality Tequila is most often made from piñas that have been cooked in clay ovens. The juice that is produced is fermented and is then ready to be distilled. Distillation varies from copper pot stills to sleek continuous stills, but the highest-quality Tequilas come from a double distillation in copper pot stills.

Typically, smooth-tasting, herbaceous 100-percent agave Tequilas are of significantly higher quality than mixtos and, therefore, cost more. Most mixtos are perfectly suitable for mixing in cocktails, though nowadays enlightened bartenders lean towards making particularly distinctive mixed drinks with the more flavorful 100-percent agave Tequilas.

Tequila sales continue to steadily grow in the United States (up 8.6 percent in 2004 and 7.7 percent in 2005) and far overshadow the comparatively meager sales of mescal. While the prime motivational force behind this reality continues to be the margarita cocktail, consumers in increasing numbers are enjoying boutique, artisanal, handcrafted premium Tequilas as shots.

Considered an oddity with a naughty image before the 1990s, Tequila has become a polished mainstream libation just in the span of one generation. Legal-age drinkers now recognize Tequila brands and become fierce loyalists. Whereas a standard 750-milliliter bottle of Tequila once sold for $12 to $15, now there is a plethora of $75 ultra premium tequilas. Today, Tequila leads all premium spirits categories in dollar growth (by percentage).

Styles of Tequila

Tequila is bottled at different officially regulated classifications.

- *Blancos, platas,* **or silvers (white)** are bottled within 60 days of distillation and therefore offer the most essential agave flavors.

- *Joven abocado* is immature Tequila that is flavored with caramel and is almost always a mixto.

- *Reposados* **(rested)** have been aged from two to twelve months in oak barrels and are favored by Mexican consumers.

- *Añejo* **(old)** are matured in oak barrels for a minimum of 12 months but no more than 36 months.

- **Extra aged,** a new category, is Tequila that has been matured in oak for at least three years.

Virtually all tequilas are bottled at 40 percent alcohol by volume (80-proof). Tequilas in the premium ($20 and up) and super-premium ranges (more than $30) have benefited both from advanced technology and modern distilling philosophies and, as such, are acknowledged by spirits experts as being clean-drinking, cultured spirits of world-class stature. One final item about Tequila: Unlike some cheaper brands of mescal, no authentic made-in-Mexico (*hecho en Mexico*) Tequilas have worms in the bottles. Tequilas, in fact, have never contained worms in the bottle.

What is mescal?

Tequila and mescal have inherent differences in pedigree, place of origin, and essence. Mescal, by contrast, is made from any of five agave varieties rather than the one blue agave, as in the case of Tequila. The workhorse variety in the making of mescal is *Agave angustifolia Haw*, which is known to Mexican farmers as *espadin*. The five non-blue agave types are one pivotal reason for mescal's marked taste difference from smoother, silkier Tequila.

Mescal production originates in primitive factories called *palenques* that are located in the five south-central Mexican states of Oaxaca, Durango, San Luis Potasi, Guerrero, and Zacatecas. Alcohol-by-volume content of mescal ranges from a low of 40-percent up to a high of 47.5 percent in more specialized bottlings.

Generally speaking, mescal follows the same production processes as Tequila. While mescal does not use the blue agave of Tequila, the greatest differences between these two drinks is not the type of agave plant used, but the method by which the piña of the agave plant is roasted or cooked and the distillation method.

For mescal, piñas are usually roasted in an earth and stone pit, which explains its smoky flavors, while Tequila uses piñas cooked in clay ovens. Likewise, Tequilas have nearly always been double-distilled in pot stills, while mescals for decades were—and to large measure still are—distilled only once. This means that many natural chemical compounds and oils remain in the finished product. These are thought in some quarters to be negative traits of mescal, giving off musky odors reminiscent of burning tires, rotting meat, or creosote. For many, mescal still has the same image that Tequila had in the 1970s and 1980s: an arcane and obscure south-of-the-border spirit with a wicked attitude.

Mescal proponents argue that these biochemical remnants are what make mescal so special and unique, and refreshingly different from Tequila. The champions of mescal claim that mescal is more authentic than Tequila because its chemical properties aren't stripped away through distillation.

That said, more than a few of the better, pricier mescals are now twice distilled and, because of that change, are cleaner tasting. Many mescals, however, remain single-distilled. The mescal distillers looking to appeal to finicky American consumers have, to some degree, also stopped placing a *gusano*, or worm, in their mescals. Only the low-end brands that trade off their outlaw images, like Monte Albán, Gusano Rojo, and the most traditional distillers, continue with that practice. A very good brand called Scorpion includes a small scorpion in its bottles for good measure.

In their hunt for business in the United States market-place, mescals have become surprisingly specialized as demand has gradually grown. There are even so-called "single village" mescals bottled under the Del Maguey label. These highly idiosyncratic mescals come from individual municipal locations in Oaxaca. Other high-end mescals are being matured in oak barrels for periods as long as five or more years. Will mescal eventually evolve to the point where it will become the next, well, Tequila? Many mescal aficionados hope not.

The message from mescal distillers is simple: mescals

are different from Tequilas and that's their heritage and primary virtue. Many mescal supporters contend that Tequilas have become too neat and tidy in their ascent to international fame and, thus, have in the process become boringly homogenized. While that might be a calculated ploy on the part of mescal producers to draw distinction between their distillates and Tequila, there is no denying that Tequila has become the large revenue "establishment" of Mexico's spirits industry.

Mescals are coming of age and may in time compete with their high-class cousins in terms of market acceptance similar to the way that France's Armagnacs have won over a fair number of brandy lovers who once thought that Cognac was the ultimate grape-based spirit.

Hecho en Mexico

While Tequila and mescal producers are keen to protect the integrity of their place names, the U.S. government has so far resisted these attempts. The U.S. absorbs 78 percent of the exports of mescals and Tequila. At this time, the words "Tequila" and "mescal" are not protected in the U.S. market, and spirits that should be considered fraudulent are sold openly in the U.S.

Proof of authenticity comes in the words "Hecho en Mexico" on the bottle as well as by a NOM number, such as NOM 1499 CRT. NOM stands for *Norma Oficial Mexicana* and is the official number given to each Tequila distillery by the Mexican government. Every genuine bottle of Tequila must identify the originating distillery. As savvy consumers, always make certain that these two identifying data are on every bottle you purchase.

Rum
History of rum

All rums are made from the tall grass known as sugarcane. No one can be certain of the origins of rum. Alexander the Great reportedly came across sugarcane, circa 300 B.C.E., in India and called it "the grass that gives honey without bees." As history's earliest distillers were probably located in the India-Pakistan region, sugarcane distillate may very well have been the first spirit to run off crude ceramic pot stills.

Rum's modern history, however, begins with Christopher Columbus's second voyage in 1493 to the Caribbean. On his initial voyage in 1492, the enterprising Columbus

A mojito is made with light rum, lime juice, simple syrup, mint sprigs, and club soda: the perfect warm-weather drink.

realized that the tropical climate of the Caribbean region held significant promise for crops such as sugarcane. The first plantings were on the island of Hispaniola, what is today Haiti and Dominican Republic.

But it would be a century and a half later that distillation of sugarcane juice and molasses, a by-product of sugar refining, would become a secondary industry to sugar refining. Barbados became the epicenter of rum distilling in the mid-seventeenth century. By the time the American colonies were operating from Maine to the Carolinas in the early eighteenth century, rum was poised to take its next big step as a trade commodity.

The naming of sugarcane distillate most likely comes from the Latin word for sugarcane, *saccharum officinarum*. Along the way, rum's been known as "rumbullion," "rumbustion," "rumbowling," and, of course, the hands-down favorite, "kill-devil." American colonists imported huge volumes of already distilled rum as well as massive quantities of molasses in order to produce rum in exchange for a multitude of North American-generated goods, such as tobacco, linens, fruits, and grains. By the time of the Revolutionary War, rum was a major business throughout the Caribbean region and an important source of revenue.

The sugarcane plantations and, by extension, rum distillers, also cultivated the slave trade, which included traders in western Africa, Great Britain, the Caribbean, and the newly independent United States. This unholy alliance thrived on the lives of countless hundreds of thousands of Africans for centuries before it was stopped. Today, rum is a vibrant segment of the beverage alcohol industry with global implications of the more positive kind.

What is Rum?

Rum is made from a mash of either sugarcane juice or molasses. The mash is first fermented, then distilled. With rum being produced in so many nations (the U.S., Haiti, Dominican Republic, Barbados, Jamaica, Bermuda, Puerto Rico, Martinique, Guadeloupe, Grenada, Guyana, Venezuela, Nicaragua, Guatemala, the Philippines, U.S. Virgin Islands, Trinidad-Tobago and Australia, to name the most prominent), there exists no worldwide governing body to oversee production or to set standards of aging and classifications. Consequently, it's up to every rum-producing country to establish production guidelines for itself. This type of self-regulating situation unfortunately plays against rum's global image.

Most rums are bottled devoid of color, neither stored in oak barrels nor matured. Puerto Rico is an exception,

Rum and cachaça are both made from the juice of sugarcane, which is a major crop in the Caribbean.

where by law, all rums must be aged in barrels for a minimum of one year. In most rum-producing locations, a relatively small percentage of rum production is matured in oak barrels for longer than one year.

The biggest differences that exist in the more expensive premium and super-premium rum lines are drawn from the use of raw materials. In other words, which type of sugarcane product does the distiller utilize: sugarcane juice or molasses?

That determination comes down largely to tradition. The French-speaking Caribbean area rum nations, like Martinique and Guadeloupe, prefer to employ freshly pressed sugarcane juice while those countries with long-held British (think Barbados, Jamaica, Bermuda) or Spanish connections (Puerto Rico, Dominican Republic) tend to use molasses, an easily attainable sugar refining by-product that is thick, gooey, and dark brown.

Rums distilled from pressed sugarcane juice are called *rhum agricole* in French. They are routinely grassy, earthy, and even herbal in character and as such are delightfully distinct, even idiosyncratic from distillery to distillery. Those made from molasses offer a stunningly wide menu of aromas, textures and tastes. The British style is typically robust, deeply flavored and intense while the Spanish style tends to be lighter and more elegant.

Naturally, the kind of still used likewise affects the character. Rums from pot still distillation are more vertically inclined, meaning they have greater depth and more layers than the horizontally inclined rums distilled in column stills.

Since, as mentioned earlier, there are no international standards for rum, the beverage alcohol industry itself loosely classifies rum five varieties.

• **White rums** are completely transparent and if produced from molasses are caney, sweet, and light. Rhum agricole white rums offer greater substance and tend to be more bittersweet than candy-shop sweet.

• **Gold rums** usually are white rums that have had caramel added to them to introduce a tint of amber tone for appearance's sake.

• **Dark rums** can be rums that have spent several years in oak barrels, deriving their color from the wood, or can be rums that have extra caramel added to them to make them look older.

• **Spiced rums** are those that have flavorings purposely added to them, like cinnamon, vanilla, nutmeg, orange rind, lemon peel, or honey.

• **Overproof rums** are those high-alcohol rums (75 percent or more alcohol) that have either not been reduced with water or minimally reduced in alcoholic strength. These high-octane rums are popular throughout the Caribbean with the locals who prefer them to rums bottled at 40-percent alcohol (80-proof).

The Cachaça File
What is Cachaça?

Cachaça is Brazil's native spirit made from sugarcane and is different from rum in that it is earthier, less sweet, spicier, and more herbal than rum. The Portuguese, who ruled Brazil from 1494 to 1822, reportedly distilled the first batches of cachaça. It evolved independently of rum alongside the massive sugarcane industry during their colonial period to become a unique regional product and should not be labeled as a variety of rum.

Produced only from sugarcane juice and not the more deeply flavored molasses, cachaça is bottled in a range of from 38 to 51 percent alcohol by volume. Next to beer, cachaça is Brazil's most consumed alcoholic beverage, averaging about 350 million gallons per year, or roughly two gallons per Brazilian. Today, there are as many as 30,000 small distillers of cachaça scattered around South America's largest country in addition to the mammoth industrial distillers.

Cachaça comes in three fundamental classifications: unaged, aged, and yellow.

• **Unaged cachaças** usually spend a year in wood barrels.

• **Aged cachaças** spend from two to twelve years in barrels.

• **Yellow cachaças** are young spirits that have caramel or wood extracts added to them to make them appear older.

Brazilians prefer to employ native woods for their cooperage, including imburana, freijo, cedar, jequitiba, and cherry. These native woods impart unique, sometimes resiny flavors to the spirits, making them exotic and delicious.

CHAPTER THREE

The Whiskeys of the World

Pot-stilled malt whisky, made of barley, water, and yeast, was the only type of whisky produced in Scotland prior to the 1830s.

All whiskeys are comprised of three fundamental base material parts: water, yeast, and grain. Seems simple—at least on the surface. Yet the broad and distinctive differences among the whiskey types from various nations come into play through a half-dozen complicated channels: different grains; types of oak barrels; time of maturation; the quality of local water; the regional environmental impact; method of distillation; and the local whiskey production regulations. Even warm versus cool climates, or inland distilleries versus seaside distilleries can have a profound effect on the resulting spirit.

These six factors individually influence each whiskey's underlying character. The best way to understand the ancient realm of whiskey is to take a tour of the world's foremost whiskey-making nations.

The word whiskey is derived from the Gaelic term for "water of life," *uisge beatha*. Complicating matters is the confusing use of the spellings "whiskey" and "whisky." Ireland and the U.S., with some exceptions like Maker's Mark Bourbon, prefer the employment of the "e," while Canada and Scotland drop the "e." The plurals then become "whiskeys" for whiskey and "whiskies" for whisky. When referring to the global industry, use "whiskey."

Whiskeys of the British Isles
The Irish whiskey file

Based on a combination of common sense, circumstantial evidence, and sketchy recordings, Ireland appears to be whiskey's homeland.

The first millennium Scots-Gaels who inhabited Ireland were known to be avid and adept brewers of dark ales made from oats and barley. Once distillation was introduced to the island, circa 1050 to1100, some brewers became distillers as well. In a vague, if tantalizing, passage from British soldiers who occupied parts of Ireland in the twelfth century, they mention the Scots-Gaels producing a strong beverage made from "boiling," implying that they used distillation. It stands to reason that the Scots-Gaels were likely boiling their ales in crude pot stills to produce crystalline uisge beathas.

Whatever the situation, by the 1500s, distilling was widespread in Ireland. By the mid-eighteenth century, there were as many as 2,000 pot stills operating throughout the island. During the 1800s, Irish whiskey was considered the international gold standard and was admired worldwide. North America evolved into Ireland's prime export destination, as drinkers of Irish descent in Canada and America yearned for a taste of their beloved Eire.

Trouble for the Irish distilling industry began with the outbreak of World War I, which closed down shipping lanes in the northern Atlantic Ocean because of U-boat activity. Once the hostilities abated in 1918, America was close to enacting the Eighteenth Amendment, which made the production, sale, and transportation of alcohol illegal within the U.S. Prohibition ran from 1919 to 1933 when it was repealed by the Twenty-First Amendment. This infamous "double whammy" of World War I and Prohibition effectively shut down Ireland's main whiskey export market and virtually destroyed the entire Irish whiskey trade in the process.

Then came the Great Depression followed by World War II. By the end of the Second World War, Americans had completely forgotten about Irish whiskey and turned instead to American-made blended whiskeys and Bourbon, as well as Scotch whisky.

At present, there are three distilleries on the island, two in the Irish Republic (Cooley in County Louth and Midleton in County Cork) and one in Northern Ireland (Old Bushmills in County Antrim). The good news is that Irish whiskey is currently on the rebound as sales have increased markedly over the last decade.

Copper pot stills in the stillhouse of the Old Bushmills Distillery in Northern Ireland

What is Irish whiskey?

There are four basic types of Irish whiskey.

• **Single malt whiskey.** This type is made from 100-percent malted barley in a pot still by a single distillery. Single malts are known for their distinctive flavors.

• **Grain whiskey.** Produced in column stills, grain whiskey is made from wheat or corn and is normally lighter than single-malt or pure pot still whiskeys.

• **Blended whiskey.** This variety is a combination of grain and single-malt whiskeys.

• **Pure pot still whiskey.** Unique to Ireland, pure pot still whisky is made from a combination of 100-percent malted and unmalted barley and is distilled in a pot still, resulting in a very potent and robust drink.

All Irish whiskeys by law must be aged for a minimum of three years in barrels, and most are distilled three times to promote extra smoothness and drinkability.

The Scotch whisky file

Christian monks exported the system of distillation along with Christianity from Ireland to Scotland by the four-teenth century, possibly earlier. The initial substantiation of its existence on the island of Britain, however, didn't occur until the last years of the fifteenth century. A Scottish Exchequer Roll recorded in 1494 that Friar John Cor of the Benedictine Lindores Abbey in Fife made a rather sizable purchase of barley malt in the amount of "viii bolls" for the purpose of making *aqua vitae*.

Since a boll amounted to 140 pounds, eight bolls of malted barley topped the scales at well over half a ton. As writer Michael Brander, author of *The Original Scotch* states, "...it is clear at once that this was no small operation. Half a ton of malt producing probably in the region of 70 gallons of spirit was not required for private consumption. Obviously the monastic establishment...was distilling on no mean scale..."

By the middle of the sixteenth century, public perceptions of uisge beatha had begun to change. In addition to uisge beatha being widely employed as a medicinal liquid, it was starting to be viewed as a social libation. Legislation initiatives introduced in the Scottish Parliament in 1555 and 1579 suggest that the use of malted barley for the production of uisge beatha had greatly accelerated across Scotland in the second half of the sixteenth century. The two acts each addressed, in part, the mandatory shifting of malted barley use for making bread and brown ale and away from the distilling of uisge beatha. Poor harvests and subsequent food shortages were the reasons given by Parliamentarians for the restrictive legislation.

Doubtless, the staunchly independent Highland and island Scots scoffed at the dictates of a governing body with which they felt little, if any, connection. These initial sixteenth century Parliamentary edicts were the first of what would eventually become an onerous litany of regulation and taxation measures concerning distilling, giving rise to an unprecedented era of illegal distilling and smuggling.

The Scots' first generations of uisge beathas were distant shadows of what was to come. After all, the farmer-distillers were unschooled, and their conditions, materials, and equipment were unsophisticated and untidy. Production was minute in comparison to modern times because the era's pot stills ranged in size from a scant four to five gallons only up to, if rarely, fifty gallons. At their finest, Scotland's early whiskies were pungent, throat-grating spirits that provided a quick buzz and a brief respite from the hardships and tedium of Middle Ages Scotland. At their worst, they were bad-tasting, fierce, skull-cracking brews. Alcohol poisoning was common and sometimes resulted in unpleasant deaths.

Scotch whisky's authentic trendsetters, superstar personalities, and innovators didn't begin appearing until the 1700s. The eighteenth and nineteenth centuries brought technological advances fed by a frenzy of ideas and a hunger for profitable gain.

What is Scotch whisky?

Scotch whisky is grain, water, and yeast. At first blush, the value of this trio of commonplace substances seems modest. Though humble in worth, these individual ordinary elements become complex and extraordinary once they are carefully combined and processed.

Barley has customarily been the requisite grain for making malt whisky in Scotland. This is not because barley was the only grain that grew well in Scotland's difficult, sometimes atrocious, climate. Oats, rye, and wheat did as well. Farmer-distillers in the early days selected an ancient strain of barley that had four rows of spikelets, called *bere*, as their grain of choice. An alternative variety was two-row barley, which made smoother ales and whiskies according to some distillers, but bere proved to be their favorite.

Bere's reliably large crop yields in poor soils and rainy climates and its tendency for early ripening accommodates farmers. Before being milled, the barley is allowed to partially germinate, thereby stimulating the grain's natural starches. This partial germination breaks down the cell walls, a process called malting. Next, the malted barley is dried in kilns to halt the growth of the natural starches. The dried malted barley is then ground into powdery grist.

Water from a trusted source, such as a burn (stream) or a spring, is boiled and mixed with the malted barley grist in large metal vessels called mash tuns. Mashing converts the starches into maltose, a natural sugar. The soupy result is a walnut-colored, sweet-smelling liquid

Barley, growing in Scotland's lowlands, has been Scottish farmers' preferred grain for producing malt whisky since early distilling days.

called wort. The wort is pumped into another metal tank (the washback), and yeast is injected.

The introduction of yeast triggers fermentation, and the maltose, an innate sugar, is transformed into carbon dioxide and alcohol over the course of 48 hours. Fermentation changes the base materials into low-alcohol (7 to 8 percent), creating a "fragrant" wash that is, for all intents and purposes, beer.

The wash-beer is then moved to a kettle-like copper pot still, the wash still, and is set to boil. During the tumultuous first distillation, the vapors are forced to pass through a cold coiled pipe, or condenser, also known as a worm. Since alcohol boils at 173.1 degrees Fahrenheit and water boils at 212 degrees Fahrenheit, the wash's alcohol vaporizes well before the water, causing a separation of properties. The alcohol vapors return to liquid form while traveling through the icy cold worm. The moderate alcohol liquid (20 to 24 percent alcohol), or low wines, is pumped into the spirits still for its second distillation for further purification and to elevate the alcohol level. Following the second distillation, the condensed vapors become a high-alcohol (70 to 72 percent), limpid distillate, the spirit.

After the second distillation, the bio-chemically altered base ingredients smell, feel, and taste anything but like simple water, grain, and yeast. Through malting, mashing, fermentation and double distillation in pot stills, they unite to become one liquid substance: pure grain alcohol.

This series of events is how all Scotch malt whiskies are born. Made in small batches in pot stills, malt whiskies are the oldest type of Scotch whisky and the sole variety of whisky made in Scotland prior to the 1830s, at which point another kind of distillation, continuous distilling, introduced grain whiskies. Modern-era Scotch whisky producers utilize both kinds of distillation.

The resultant transparent liquid is deceptively compelling. When drawn fresh off the still, the virgin spirit smells strikingly similar to a damp garden in June. Dewy scents of fresh flowers, green vegetation, and pine rush at you one moment, then yeasty odors of bread dough or dry breakfast cereal grab your attention the next.

This potent, immature fluid, which registers 70 to 72 percent alcohol, initially burns the tongue if tasted undiluted. But as the taste buds adjust to the virgin alcohol's racy nature, layers of ripe fruit and grain flavors emerge. Even at this nascent stage, one can project how the razor-edged charms of the spirit can, with maturation, mellowing, and time, be transformed into an alcoholic beverage of unusual virtuosity, nuance, and complexity.

The raw spirits are next placed in oak barrels for maturation and mellowing for a legal minimum of three years. Scots have traditionally preferred used barrels, in particular those from heartland America that once held Kentucky Bourbon or Tennessee sour mash whiskey, and from southern Spain that formerly aged Sherry, Spain's fabled fortified wine. In recent years, experimentation with different varieties of used barrels has led some distillers to include barrels that once held Port and assorted wines in their cooperage inventories.

Barrels are rarely refilled more than three times because at that advanced point much of their acids (lignin,

Whisky casks and kiln house at Glendronach Distillery, Scotland

tannin, vanillin) have been leached out, rendering them useless. Barrel selection is an extremely important job, one that affects a whisky many years down the pike.

Scotch whisky styles and classifications

Since the beginnings of the continuous still in the 1820s and 1830s, there have been two distinct varieties of raw whisky made in Scotland: single-malt whisky, which is made in small batches from malted barley at a single distillery using the traditional pot still method, and grain whisky, which is made in enormous volumes from corn or wheat via the continuous distillation process in tall, metal column stills. Typically, single-malt whiskies display deeper character and individual tastes than grain whiskies. These two fundamental whisky types create the three classifications of Scotch.

• **Single-malt whisky.** This is the 100-percent malted barley whisky of one distillery distilled in a pot still, labeled under the originating distillery name. Some single-malt whiskies are labeled under the names of independent merchants who purchase barrels from single malt distilleries then bottle them under their own name.

• **Blended malt whisky (aka, vatted malt, pure malt).** A 100-percent malted barley whisky that is produced from the malt whiskies of two or more malt distilleries and labeled under a brand name.

• **Blended whisky.** A whisky that is comprised of a combination of any number of single-malt and grain whiskies and labeled under a brand name rather than a distillery name.

Also, when a Scotch whisky label declares an age, like "15 Years Old," that indicates that the youngest whisky used in the creation of that whisky was aged for no less than 15 years. There may be older whiskies in the final product.

Scotch whisky quality

Many spirits authorities believe that the whiskies of Scotland, especially the single-malt variety, offer the widest latitude and roster of smells, tastes, and textures of any spirits category. This is so for two reasons. One, the single-malt whiskies of Scotland are presently the finest grain distillates produced, possibly ever.

Two, single malts accurately reflect their places of origin like no other type of distillate, with the possible exception of Grande Champagne, Petite Champagne, and Borderies cognacs. As such, they display remarkably vivid and precise personalities.

A much better way to look at Scotland's single-malt whiskies is either as an inland whisky or as a maritime whisky. Inland whiskies (Speyside, Northern Highlands, Central Highlands, Lowlands, Western Highlands) are those that offer floral, oaky, grainy, and softly smoky qualities while maritime whiskies (distilleries on Islay, Orkney Islands, Isles of Skye, Mull, Arran, Campbeltown, or seaside locations) are salty and briny to varying degrees, reflecting the distillery's nearness to the sea.

Like a single-estate wine, chocolate, or coffee, these whiskies reflect a true *goût de terroir*, or taste of the land. This singularity and authenticity are what makes Scotland's single malts so attractive and distinctive.

Scotch on the rocks with an orange twist and a cherry

Whiskeys of North America

The U.S. whiskey file

In colonial America, the alcoholic beverages of choice were rum, applejack (apple brandy), perry (pear brandy), Madeira (the fortified wine from the Island of Madeira), and ale. Whiskey was way down on the menu because grains, except for rye, did not grow well along the eastern seaboard, where the 13 colonies abutted each other.

Whiskey-making didn't really begin in earnest in the New World until Scots-Irish and German settlers moved west into western Pennsylvania and western Maryland, places where rye flourished. In those western outposts, American whiskey came alive.

Following the Revolutionary War, America was mired in debt to the tune of more than $50 million, a gargantuan sum for the era. By 1790, the massive amounts of money loaned to us by nations like France and Spain to defeat the British were coming due. To raise cash, U.S. Treasury Secretary Alexander Hamilton and President George Washington decided to stiffly tax distilling and distilled spirits.

The farmer-distillers of Pennsylvania and Maryland revolted. Washington sent 13,000 militiamen to Pittsburgh to quell the revolt. The revolt was easily squashed, but, in the meantime, many farmer-distillers packed up in disgust and relocated in the still-virgin countryside that comprised the Ohio River Valley, especially north-central Kentucky, to escape the taxation.

What these early settlers in the 1790s found was

a remarkably fertile region where the hunting was exceptional, the Native Americans were few and one grain in particular grew like wildfire: corn.

By 1810, it is estimated that 2,000 stills were operating in Kentucky, trying to deal with the bumper crops of corn. The area that experienced the biggest explosion of distilling was Bourbon County, so named in honor of the French aristocracy that helped finance the Revolutionary War. The name stuck, as consumers wanted more of that "Bourbon whiskey."

But the biggest boost to Kentucky Bourbon whiskey came when shipping lanes opened on the Mississippi River. Once Bourbon began shipping down to New Orleans and on to the eastern port cities of Philadelphia, New York, and Boston, Bourbon whiskey was here to stay.

Another key development occurred in Kentucky in the 1830s when an innovative Scotsman by the name of Dr.

Bininger's advertising label for its Pioneer Bourbon

James Crow devised a system, which is called "sour mash," in which a portion of the fermentation, known as the "backset," is held back and added to the next mixture. This procedure promotes continuity from mash to mash.

When stocks were reduced after the Civil War, the distilling industries of Kentucky and Tennessee geared up to begin supplying whiskey to the newly opening territories west of the Mississippi. Beer and wine didn't travel well; Bourbon did. Consequently, Bourbon and Tennessee sour mash whiskey were the prime lubricants of the Wild West.

Then, like their peers in Ireland, the four-headed monster of World War I, Prohibition, the Great Depression, and World War II hamstrung American whiskey distillers. Distillery closings riddled the industry as sales slumped badly from 1915 to 1950. The markets rebounded somewhat in the 1950s.

Then whiskey distillers were adversely hit again by the dramatic growth of vodka in the 1960s and 1970s. One positive development from the 1960s was the recognition by the U.S. Congress of Bourbon's importance to America. In 1964, a congressional resolution named Bourbon "America's native spirit."

In the 1980s, things picked up once again for American whiskey with the release of high-end, more expensive bottlings made from small lots of barrels ("small-batch whiskeys") or even more exotic, whiskeys that came from a single barrel. Today, the American whiskey industry, thanks in large measure to the popularity of small-batch and single-barrel whiskeys, is thriving and healthy.

What is straight Bourbon whiskey?

While Kentucky is the traditional home and epicenter of the Bourbon industry, in truth, Bourbon can be legally produced in any state in the Union. Virginia remains a significant distilling center for Bourbon in America. Straight Bourbon whiskey is an international icon and recognized as America's hallmark distillate.

The American whiskey industry is a tightly regulated business. In order for a whiskey to become properly labeled as a straight Bourbon whiskey, it must meet a set of standards. Those regulations include:

• Straight Bourbon's grain mash must be made from at least 51 percent corn.

• Straight Bourbon must be matured in new, charred barrels for a minimum of two years.

• Straight Bourbon cannot be distilled at higher than 80 percent alcohol by volume, or 160-proof.

• Straight Bourbon whiskey can be reduced in alcoholic strength only with distilled water.

• Straight Bourbon whiskey must be bottled at least 40 percent alcohol by volume, or 80-proof.

• As a straight whiskey, it is unlawful to add any color or flavor enhancements.

Bourbon distillation usually involves an initial distillation in a column still and a second pass in a pot still-like kettle called a "doubler" or a "thumper" (because of the pounding noises these stills make during distillation). So America's foremost whiskeys are double-distilled, for all intents and purposes.

Unlike Irish and Scottish (and, as we shall see in a

few pages, Canadian distillers), American distillers must by law employ unused barrels for aging their whiskeys. Barrels must also be charred on the inside. Charring levels of one-to-four are the norm, with level four being the deepest char. The deeper char levels influence the new spirit more than lighter char levels, imparting smells and tastes of caramel, maple, or vanilla.

Bourbon warehouses are known as "rickhouses" and populate north-central Kentucky by the scores. The aging period in Kentucky is generally much shorter than in cooler climates, like those of Ireland and Scotland. Spirits mature much faster in warm, humid conditions than in cool, damp climates and so can be bottled sooner.

What Is Tennessee sour mash whiskey?

Tennessee sour mash whiskey is very close in production methods to straight Bourbon except for a filtration process, called the Lincoln County process, in which the whiskey is dripped through chunks of maple charcoal in huge vats. This happens after distillation and prior to the aging.

Ten feet deep, the charcoal is so densely packed that it takes each drip many hours to make it to the bottom. The idea is to leach out any impurities not stripped away by distillation. The result is a smoky type of whiskey that is reminiscent of cigarette ashes or chimney soot.

Because of the inclusion of the Lincoln County process step, law does not allow Tennessee sour mash whiskeys to be identified as "Bourbon." This is no hardship for the Tennessee distillers, who prefer to be known as makers of fine Tennessee sour mash whiskey. After

The Jack Daniel's Distillery in Tennessee, 1949

enjoying a rich history of distilling, only two distilleries still exist in Tennessee, Jack Daniel's and George Dickel.

What is rye whiskey?

Aside from being the first important type of American whiskey, rye whiskey is variety admired among distillers. It differs from Bourbon with its peppery, less sweet flavor, and it's made with at least 51-percent rye in the U.S.

Rye whiskey faded in the deluge of available bourbons in the nineteenth century. After the repeal of Prohibition in 1933, a handful of rye whiskey brands reappeared, but again the category flagged against the unstoppable tide of Bourbon. By the 1970s and 1980s rye whiskey was scarcely seen.

Following the turn of the third millennium, more rye whiskeys started becoming available as word spread about this variety's pedigree, historical importance, and status within the American distilling industry. At present, there are more straight rye whiskeys in the marketplace that at any time since the early twentieth century.

What is North American blended whiskey?

Following World War II, a genuine phenomenon occurred in the North American whiskey category spurred by Sam Bronfman, the CEO of Canada-based drinks giant Joseph E. Seagram: inexpensive and ubiquitous blended American and blended Canadian whiskeys. Two Seagram brands ruled supreme from the late 1940s through to the mid-1970s, Seagram's 7 Crown from the U.S. and Seagram's VO from Canada.

These easy-drinking whiskeys are blends of 20-percent straight whiskey and 80-percent neutral grain spirits. Both are wood-aged. While they lack the depth of character and elegance of straight Bourbon, Tennessee sour mash whiskey, and straight rye whiskey, they nonetheless serve a noble purpose as excellent mixers.

The Canadian whisky file

Canada's first licensed distillery opened in 1769. Large numbers of Scottish and Irish immigrants who entered Canada in the nineteenth century brought with them a natural thirst for good whisky. Column-still distillation is the driving force, as is a philosophy that focuses on the art of blending.

The acknowledged thumbprint character of almost all Canadian whiskies is their delightful drinkability. Canadian whiskies are designed, first and foremost, to

Whiskey in shooter glasses

be smooth and approachable. In light of the 200 million bottles that are produced each year, one would have to draw the conclusion that this approach has worked out.

Canadian whiskies are typically made from a majority of corn and lesser portions of rye and barley. Canadian whiskies are matured in barrels for a legal minimum of three years. Interestingly, as opposed to the rigors of governmentally imposed production regulations south of the border in the U.S., Canada's whisky industry is largely self-regulated and is thus a significant departure from other whiskey-making nations. This liberal system has triumphed for a century and a half as Canadian whiskies have flourished globally and have come to be viewed as reliable and welcome libations. On top of having first-class entrée on an international scale, the gentle, mildly sweet nature of Canadian whiskies makes them prime ingredients in scores of whiskey cocktails.

Two pivotal companies, Hiram Walker and Joseph E. Seagram, led the charge in the nineteenth century and their brands still dominate to this day. In recent years, however, smaller distilleries, like Forty Creek in Ontario and Glenora in Nova Scotia, have raised the bar in terms of offering more idiosyncratic whiskies.

Other whiskeys of the world: Pacific Rim and Central Asia

Thriving whiskey industries reside in Japan, New Zealand, and India. After World War II, the spread of western culture in Asia triggered keen interest in whiskey. Two large and ambitious firms dominate the Japanese whiskey trade: Suntory and Nikka. In terms of style, Japanese whiskeys tend to resemble those produced in Scotland in their dryness and the use of malted barley.

New Zealand's offerings are more modest, while India has developed one of the most vigorous and successful whiskey industries in the world, pumping out numerous brands, some of which are similar to Scotland's and America's whiskeys.

Whiskey has evolved into an authentic global industry of the first rank.

CHAPTER FOUR

The Brandies of the World

Cognac, a double-distilled brandy from France, has gained worldwide popularity.

While whiskeys are grain-based, brandies are generally fruit-based spirits. In other words, before one creates a brandy, one needs first to ferment a wine. Indeed, the word "brandy" is derived from the Dutch term for "burnt wine," *brandewijn*.

The brandy category covers a startlingly wide spectrum of distillates, from customary grape spirits (Cognac, Armagnac, American alembic brandy, Spanish brandy, and Brandy de Jerez, pisco) to apple spirits (Calvados, applejack) to grape pomace spirits (grappa, marc) to orchard and vine fruit spirits (*eaux-de-vie*) to rare flower oil spirits made in northern Italy.

The first brandies were developed in the Middle Ages in Europe and were unaged, raw, biting spirits such as primitive grappas. The sixteenth and seventeenth centuries brought wood-aging to production, especially in Holland, Britain, and France, which everything changed for the better. The wood influence vastly improved the harsh, fresh-off-the-still liquids, making them far more palatable.

Today, brandy is produced just about anywhere wine is made. It's best to cover this intriguing and sprawling category country by country.

France

Merchants, brokers, and shippers in sixteenth century Holland described France's growing number of distilled wines as *brandewijns*, and the English altered the Dutch term to *brandy*. Brandies are the quintessence of the wines from which they are produced.

Many other wine-producing countries have made brandy in the last 500 years. But since the mid-seventeenth century, no nation has provided more world-class brandies than France. Of the dozen prime beverage alcohol *Appellation d'Origine Contrôlée* regions defined by the French government's *Institut National des Appellations d'Origine* (INAO), three—Calvados in Normandy, Armagnac in Gascony, and Cognac in the Charente-Maritime—specialize in brandy. Cognac and Armagnac are grape brandies while Calvados is comprised of apples, and sometimes, apples and pears.

All Cognacs are brandies, but not all brandies are Cognacs. Armagnac is not a type of Cognac, but rather a type of brandy. Cognac is brandy made in the region bearing the same name; therefore not all brandies from around the globe are Cognac. The confusion comes from Cognac being so closely associated with brandy that they can seem one and the same to the consumer.

Armagnac is a unique category of grape-based distillate that comes from a distinct region, as does Cognac. They are both French, but there the similarities end. Let's forge ahead and discuss what makes each of these three superb brandies from France so singular, sought-after, and luscious.

The Cognac file: What is Cognac?

Cognac, the most international and successful of France's brandy trio, is the double-distilled brandy made from grapes that originate in the west-central region known as Charente-Maritime. Remarkably, ninety percent of the region's 25,000 farms grow grapes. Brandy production at some level of grape-growing, distillery work, glass production, packaging, and barrel making, puts money into the pockets of 40,000 Cognaçais. Global sales of Cognac in more than 160 nations keep these people busy.

The French government has demarcated six grape-growing areas that fan out in irregular concentric circles from the core cities of Cognac, Jarnac, and Segonzac. The bulls-eye district is Grande Champagne, whose friable, chalky soils produce grapes that, when fermented and distilled, turn into long-lived brandies of great distinction. Approximately 13,000 hectares (or 32,110 acres) in Grande Champagne are devoted to cultivating the grapes that make Cognac.

Cradling Grande Champagne are the larger Petite Champagne district (16,000 hectares or 39,520 acres under vine), and the compact Borderies district (4,000 hectares or 9,880 acres). Both are renowned for their outstanding, deeply flavorful brandies, with Petite Champagne being the more fruit-driven of the two and Borderies typically featuring lovely walnut-like qualities.

Encircling Grande Champagne, Petite Champagne, and Borderies is Fins Bois, a vast area of limestone soils that covers over 350,000 hectares, 33,000 of which are planted to vineyard. Around Fins Bois lies the even

A Cognac bottling factory in France. France maintains strict laws governing the production of Cognac to ensure a refined and consistent product.

bigger Bons Bois (386,000 hectares or roughly 954,000 acres). The least crucial in terms of quality impact is Bois à Terroir, which sits at ocean's edge on the Atlantic. In all, a total of nearly 80,000 hectares/197,600 acres are under vine in the six districts.

One of the distinctions of Cognac is the use of a copper pot still called the Charentais still. French law dictates that Charentais stills may not hold more than 690 gallons. Small pot stills like these distill spirits of high quality and individuality. To achieve the cleanest spirits, the Cognaçais distill twice, but as decreed by law, at never higher than 72 percent alcohol. The lower the alcohol, the more character that remains.

The French government's tightly controlled production laws also demand that distillation of any fall grape harvest must be completed by March 31 of the succeeding year.

Once the fresh spirits (referred to as *eaux-de-vie*) are drawn off the pot still, they are placed in French oak barrels (from oak typically harvested from the Limousin and Tronçais forests) that hold 75 to 125 gallons for maturation.

The interaction of the raw spirit and the oils, acids, and chemical compounds of the wood under ideal conditions causes the gradual transformation of the *eaux-de-vie* into Cognac. By law, the *eaux-de-vie* must age in barrels for two years. Of course, during maturation there is some evaporation of the alcohol. In Cognac, evaporation consumes at least 20 million barrels per year.

Cognac is the most refined and consistent of France's three brandy varieties in part, because of the industry's faithful adherence to the craft of blending. By combining different brandies, the Cognaçais claim that they are able to accentuate the virtues of the many into a reliable product of towering quality.

The Armagnac File: What is Armagnac?

If Cognac is the brandy equivalent of a Bentley, Armagnac is a Jeep Wrangler. Whereas the Cognaçais reach for consistency, elegance, and high quality, the Armagnaçais aspire to surprise, challenge, and delight consumers through big flavors, idiosyncrasy, and high quality. Some consumers say that they prefer Cognac to Armagnac because of these philosophical differences (meaning, steadfastness versus precociousness) while others rave about the sensory adventure that Armagnac inherently brings.

Armagnac is the brandy of France's bucolic southwest region known as Gascony, home to the Musketeers, foie gras, and green, rolling hills. Like its distant cousin Cognac, Armagnac is distilled grape wine and is aged in oak barrels.

Armagnac boasts three brandy districts. Bas-Armagnac contributes 57 percent of all brandy production in Gascony from its sandy and silty soils, creating a delicate, elegant, and fruity drink. Tenarèze accounts for 40 percent of production and is noted for its clay/limestone soils and robust, long-lived brandies. Last is Haut-Armagnac, from which a mere 3 percent of production is contributed. Whereas a century ago vineyards could be seen around every turn in the lane, these three areas in 2007 total only 15,000 hectares, or 37,050 acres of vineyard land.

Distillation in Armagnac occurs mostly in November and December of the harvest year. As opposed to the small pot stills employed in Cognac in which brandies are double-distilled, the Armagnaçais opt for the more efficient column stills that run continuously in a single distillation process for 95 percent of their brandies. The remaining 5 percent are distilled in smaller pot stills. The single distillation method means that the brandies of Armagnac are stouter in nature than those made in Cognac because fewer of the natural chemical compounds have been stripped away.

Interestingly, only a handful of Gascon Armagnac producers distill their own brandy. They prefer instead to employ roving distillers who have column stills mounted on wheeled platforms. The roving distillers move from farm to farm distilling each grower's wines.

Maturation happens in black oak barrels in Armagnac for a legal minimum of two years. Armagnac also specializes in vintage releases, meaning bottlings produced from the grapes of one particular harvest. These brandies especially showcase the peculiarities and virtues of individual vintage years in ways that blended brandies can never do. While the overwhelming majority of Cognac is exported around the world, most annual production of Armagnac, 65 percent, remains within France. The rest is exported to more than 130 nations.

If one truth can sum up the Cognac-Armagnac rivalry, it would be this: The breadth of Armagnac's list of characteristics is broader than that of Cognac. When Armagnac is in top form, it is as exciting and compelling as any of the world's foremost aged spirits.

Armagnac stills at Distillerie Lafontan, France

The Calvados File: What is Calvados?

Calvados is the world's finest apple and apple-pear brandy. It comes from Normandy in France's northwest corner, which has the perfect climate and precipitation, soil types, and topography for fruit orchards. Calvados is defined as a distilled spirit made either from cider apples or a marriage of cider apples and perry pears.

Calvados production dates back to the sixteenth century when the Normans started boiling their apple ciders in pot stills to produce spirits. After harvesting in the autumn, apples are pressed and the juice is fermented into cider. The cider is then distilled and the resultant crystal-clear spirits are placed in oak barrels ranging in size from

Calvados on display at a shop in Honfleur, France

220 to 400 liters or huge vats that can hold up to 6,000 liters.

The Calvados region is demarcated into three brandy-making districts. The largest is designated as "Calvados;" here the brandies are created out of apple cider in column stills from one distillation. The apple brandies labeled under this classification are generally good, but lacking in distinction.

Brandies from the hallowed "Calvados Pays d'Auge" district, on the other hand, are to Calvados what Grande Champagne, Petite Champagne, and Borderies brandies are to Cognac—the best of the best. These frequently exquisite and delicate brandies are double-distilled in copper pot stills and, consequently, offer far more depth of character and the chance of longer life than those labeled only as Calvados. Minimum aging in oak barrels or vats is two years in these two districts. Calvados Pays d'Auge brandies are for serious aficionados.

The third district is Domfrontais, an official designation that was created only a decade ago. As opposed to Calvados and Calvados Pays d'Auge, at least 30 percent of the juice must come from pears. The combination of apple and pear makes Domfrontais brandies concentrated and fruitier than those from the apple-dominant districts. The minimum maturation in oak for Domfrontais is three years.

Overlooked aspects of Calvados include its wonderful application in cooking and baking and also as a sophisticated palate cleanser between courses of a meal. Likewise in the new cocktail era, Calvados makes a smashing ingredient in mixed drinks like the Jack Rose, the Big Apple Martini, and the Normandy Cooler.

Understanding French brandy labels and classifications

Different legal classifications for Armagnac, Calvados, and Cognacs are defined by age and the amount of time that brandies have spent maturing in oak barrels. Though consumer fascination with pricier vintage and single-barrel bottlings is growing, the overwhelming majority of all three types of French brandy are blended for V.S.(Very Special), V.S.O.P. (Very Superior Old Pale) and X.O. (Extra Old) varieties.

Here are the legal breakdowns for aging:

- **Armagnac V.S.:** 2-year minimum in barrels
- **Armagnac V.S.O.P.:** 5-year minimum
- **Armagnac X.O.:** 6-year minimum
- **Armagnac Hors d'Age:** 10-year minimum
- **Armagnac Vintage:** Grapes must all come from the harvest year displayed on the label.
- **Calvados Fine/Three Stars:** 2-year minimum in barrels
- **Calvados Vieux/Réserve:** 3-year minimum
- **Calvados V.O./Vieille Réserve/V.S.O.P.:** 4-year minimum
- **Calvados Extra/X.O./Napoleon/Hors d'Age/Age Inconnu:** 6-year minimum
- **Cognac V.S./Three Stars:** 2-year minimum in barrels
- **Cognac V.SO.P.:** 4-year minimum
- **Cognac X.O./Hors d'Age/Napoleon/Extra:** 6-year minimum
- **Cognac Vintage:** Grapes must all come from the harvest year displayed on the label.

What is marc?

Marc (pronounced *mahr*) is the French equivalent of Italy's grappa. They are both made from the spent grape pomace left over after winemaking. The pomace is pressed to obtain any remaining grape juice. That grape juice is then fermented and distilled. Rarely is marc ever placed in wood barrels for aging. The point of marc is to drink it fresh and unaged.

What's so attractive to wine consumers about French brandies is their undeniable relationship to the *terroir* which produced them. To the French, terroir is the sum total of the environment in which a wine or spirit is created: the soil, the water, the air. Each one is an authentic "libation of place," one that enhances a fully rounded and varied lifestyle of food, wine, and spirits.

Italy
The grappa file: What is grappa?

Grappa began as a rural alcoholic beverage, made in the late autumn after Italy's grape harvest and the making of regional wine. This genesis took place in Italy's northern provinces located near the Alps around the time that the Middles Ages were ending and making way for the Renaissance (fourteenth century). Winemakers took the partially fermented by-product of wine production, the leftover juicy grape pulp, seeds, and skins, known as pomace, and sold it to traveling distillers who boiled the pomace in small, mobile copper pot stills. The intense heating created a potent vapor. When the vapor was cooled in copper coils, it condensed, becoming the crystalline, fragrant, and high-alcohol liquid called *grappa*.

Long the abrasive tipple of the peasant population that farmed Italy's countryside, grappa was fancied by its unsophisticated creators in any number of applications: as a relaxing, mood-altering elixir; as a heating fuel; as a vitamin supplement; as a restorative for weary pilgrims; as a cure for impotence; and even as a medicine for the frail and infirm.

Gulping down old-fashioned, pedal-to-the-metal grappa, though, was reason enough to stay hale and hearty. At 50- to 60-percent alcohol, the likely strength for many locally made grappas, all except the most robust country dwellers would be easily and rapidly anesthetized,

The reputation of grappa has grown in recent years, and it is now known as an elegant *digestivo*.

despite the terrible taste. Flavorings like honey, flowers, and herbs were commonly added to primitive grappas to help mitigate their oily, harsh flavor. Sometimes water was added to lessen the impact of the elevated percentages of alcohol. By the eighteenth century, grappa was being produced in most provinces on the Italian peninsula.

After being publicly maligned for decades as the lowbrow cousin of the more elegant European brandies, such as France's Cognacs, Armagnacs, fruit brandies called *eaux-de-vie*, and even its own pomace-based spirit relation known as marc, grappa needed a makeover. Modern-era grappa producers in the early 1980s said, "Enough." Looming globalization and the expanding international marketplace demanded that changes first be made at the source: the producer.

The only way to combat grappa's thuggish image was to modernize and change customary production methods. A handful of Italy's master distillers, especially the Nonino family, Antonella Bocchino, Angelo Gaja, and Jacopo Poli, decided to place a heightened emphasis on quality. Their goals, made independently of one another, were to alter the international perception of their native distillate by making grappa less provincial and more cosmopolitan. In short, they each saw the dire need to create more drinkable grappa.

One of the most critical in a string of innovations was to begin distilling the pomace of individual grape types separately rather than mixing those of multiple grape varieties together.

Another advance was acknowledging the importance of capturing the essence of top-grade pomace by sourcing only the best winemaking remnants from Italy's finest vintners. These innovators also realized that they needed to distill the pomace as soon as possible to capture the innate freshness of the grapes, rather than allowing the pomace to sit around for days, stewing and fermenting on its own.

Now, grappa is no longer the butt of snide remarks and rude monikers. Distilled spirits authorities consider the new generation of grappa to be one of the finest *digestivo* brandies available. So revered, elegant, and trendy has grappa become, that it has even inspired non-Italian distillers, like northern California's highly esteemed Germain-Robin distillery, to produce their own versions of it.

Sublimely complex yet approachable, contemporary Italian grappas typically range in strength from 40 to 45-percent alcohol. The best are produced from single grape varieties cultivated on single estates. A growing number are matured in wood barrels made of oak, juniper, birch, ash, cherry, or acacia. Some are flavored with natural flavorings such as chamomile, rue leaves, quinine, anise, pine nuts, rhubarb, almonds, cinnamon, mint, cloves, juniper, and caraway seeds.

No longer the favored spirit of only alpine Italy (Friuli-Venezia Giulia, Trentino-Alto Adige, Veneto, and Piedmont), fine grappas hail from such central and southern provinces as Tuscany, Umbria, Campania, Sardinia, Sicily, Basilicata, and The Marches. Truth is, thanks to the vision of a handful of determined distillers in the 1970s and 1980s, grappa has, with justification, gripped Italy and the cultured culinary world.

Iberian Peninsula
Spain

The majority of Spanish brandies are produced from Airén grapes grown in the vast vineyards of La Mancha in central Spain. Many Airén vines, in fact, are trained to grow on pergolas placed above other crops. Spanish brandies are usually dark, rich, and a touch sweet.

The most famous Spanish brandy of all is Brandy de Jerez. Spanish law dictates that it must be matured in Sherry barrels in the Sherry-making district (also known as the "Sherry Triangle," bounded by the cities of Jerez de la Frontera, Puerto de Santa Maria, and Sanlúcar de Barrameda), located in Andalusia in the south of Spain. Sherry producers have been distilling since at least the

A tulip-shaped Spanish *copita*, ideal for serving brandies and whiskeys. The narrow mouth funnels subtle aromas upward during a tasting.

sixteenth century, if only as additives to their export wine to preserve the wine. Brandy de Jerez is Spain's sole officially demarcated brandy district.

Spanish brandies are distilled in both column stills and pot stills. As a matter of routine and custom, they are aged in an ingenious maturation system that mirrors the system utilized for aging Sherry: the *solera* system. The solera system calls for a pyramid architecture where the ground floor row of barrels contains the oldest brandies and the next row above the ground floor row is a little younger and so on. The ground floor row is called the solera while the upper rows are known as *criaderas*.

When producers need to bottle more supply, they dip into the oldest brandies from the solera, but draw no more than one-third of the barrel's content. Younger brandy from the row of barrels directly above replaces the older brandy from the ground floor and so on up the pyramid. The inherent beauty of the solera system is that you are always marrying older brandies with newer, fresher ones. The older brandies lend depth to the younger ones and the younger ones bring vigor to the older ones.

Aside from Brandy de Jerez, there are several brandies made in the wine regions that surround Barcelona, most prominently, Penedes.

Portugal

Situated in western Portugal's Estremadura district near the city of Lisbon lies Lourinhã, Portugal's lone officially demarcated brandy-making district. The region's grape-based brandy is called *aguardente*. While respected and liked in Portugal, it is not well known in North America.

North America
United States

Brandy has been made in America since the time of the California missions. Up until the 1980s, however, most of America's brandies were eminently forgettable and lacking in distinctive qualities. These faceless, mass-produced brandies were all distilled in column stills in huge volumes.

Then in the 1980s a small group of brandy mavericks from the western states started to make small batches of

Still room of RMS Brandy, Napa, California

high quality brandies in small pot stills called alembics. This group included Hubert Germain-Robin and Ansley Coale, Jr. of Germain-Robin of Mendocino County, California; Steve McCarthy of Clear Creek Distillery in Portland, Oregon; and George Rupf of St. George Spirits of Alameda County, California. Their efforts changed the face of brandy-making in America for the better with their commitment to offer unusual and luscious brandies, *eaux-de-vie*, fruit liqueurs, and grappas year after year.

Now, even the companies that flourished from producing millions of gallons of mediocre brandies from Thompson Seedless grapes grown in California's Central Valley from the mid-1930s on have begun making brandies with character and individuality that are more in keeping with European quality and standards.

South America

Pisco is the grape brandy made in both Chile and Peru. Both nations claim to be the originator, but most experts and spirits historians believe that Peru is the undisputed homeland of this disarming brandy. The widely accepted story goes that Spanish Conquistadors planted vineyards around 1600 near the Peruvian port town that today is known as Pisco and soon began distilling the wines in pot stills.

The seven favored and customary grape types are *quebranta* (a favorite of Peruvian grape growers), normal black, *mollar*, Italian grape, *moscatel*, *torontel*, and *albilla*. The last four varieties are highly perfumed and therefore make varieties that are charmingly aromatic and floral. Piscos are distilled in a variety of pot stills of different shapes and capacities.

Pisco has the distinction of being matured in porous clay jugs and cisterns rather than wood barrels or casks, allowing the spirits to oxidize precisely as they would in porous wood barrels, but without picking up wood's lignins and tannins. The resultant brandy is clear, floral, fruity, and delicate.

Pisco Sour cocktails are made from a mix of pisco, lemon juice, simple syrup, egg white, and Angostura bitters.

CHAPTER FIVE

The Liqueurs of the World

Limoncello, a lemon liqueur produced in southern Italy, uses the rind of the lemon but not the juice, which keeps it from being too tart.

The most misunderstood major category of distilled spirits among consumers is the liqueurs sector. Much of the confusion about liqueurs spawns from how these lovely spirits are best employed as part of a sophisticated contemporary lifestyle. Consumers often wonder whether to view liqueurs solely as postprandial late evening pleasures that aid digestion, and what to do with liqueurs that are often only served as ingredients in cocktails.

The best way to answer these service queries starts with comprehension of what liqueurs are and how they developed over the centuries.

The liqueur file: What is a liqueur?

By definition liqueurs (cordials has become a dated term) are alcoholic beverages that have a spirits base of grape or other fruits, grain, or vegetable, and are typically flavored with botanicals like herbs, roots, seeds, and barks; fresh and dried fruits; nuts; dairy products, cream, in particular; and spices such as cinnamon, vanilla, nutmeg, allspice, coriander, and countless others.

Flavoring in liqueurs occurs through one of four methods:

• **Percolation,** or flavor extraction through the circulating of spirits through containers holding flavoring agents

• **Infusion,** or steeping of mashed fruits or herbs in

(usually hot) water or alcohol, filtering, and mixing with spirits and sugar

• **Maceration,** or steeping of fruits or herbs in alcohol, which breaks down the fibers, and makes the fruits and herbs release their oils and juices

• **Distillation,** or the mixing of low-level alcohol and flavorings before distillation.

Each method is effective and widely employed.

The bitters truth

A host of liqueurs, commonly referred to as bitters, are viewed as appetite stimulants and are traditionally served before dinner as *apèritifs*. Italians call these light-to-moderate strength beverages (14 to 30 percent alcohol by volume), *aperitivos*. The pre-meal libation movement began in earnest in Europe in the nineteenth century. One of the first was Amer Picon, which was brought to the marketplace in the 1830s by Gaetan Picon, a French soldier fighting in Algeria. In 1840s France, Joseph Dubonnet invented his classic quinine-flavored, wine-based apèritif, Dubonnet, and Alphonse Jupperin introduced St. Raphael.

In Italy, Fernet Branca, the jet-black and particularly bitter aperitivo, was introduced in 1845 and, intriguingly, was the sole alcoholic beverage imported into the U.S. during Prohibition. Gaspare Campari bestowed his legendary and quintessential Campari bitters upon the drinking world in Milan in the 1860s. Created from a secret recipe of 68 herbs, spices, roots, citrus peels, and leaves, Campari caused a sensation in Italy that continues to this day.

Though bitter liqueurs are often consumed before meals as apèritifs, the earliest liqueurs were used as after-dinner digestifs.

Scores of other apèritifs have followed, including Rosso Antico, Lillet, Aperol, Cynar, Averna, and Byrrh. Most are served slightly chilled, 58 to 65 degrees Fahrenheit, with a twist of orange on the rocks, or, just as routinely, mixed with a few ounces of orange juice. In Italy especially, quaffing an apèritif in an outdoor establishment before dinner is part of the culture.

Digestives

Liqueurs have been around for at least six centuries. During the era of plague, dirty water, and rampant pestilence, Christian monks were the most educated members of the social structure and frequently acted as community physicians as well as spiritual shepherds. The monks recognized the dire need for consumable antidotes to commonplace illnesses like influenza and colds.

Primarily, the earliest liqueurs were created to aid with dyspepsia. Dyspepsia is derived from the Greek term *duspepsia*, which literally translates to "difficult digestion," and encompasses all sorts of social embarrassments and personal discomfort. Liqueurs that are composed of seeds, roots, leaves, and spices have assisted in digestion since the late Middle Ages.

The monks routinely created liquid concoctions by steeping a myriad of botanicals in either wine or neutral grain or fruit-based spirits. These potions were revered for their healing and restorative properties. It has been claimed that certain barks, grasses, roots, plants, seeds, and herbs can, when either chewed or included in liquids, help relieve everyday difficulties, especially with digestion. Among the most commonly utilized botanicals were saffron, sweet rush, calamus, gentian, quinine, centaury, rosemary, caraway, hyssop, sage, absinthe, aniseed, mint, and rhubarb. Honey, long recognized for

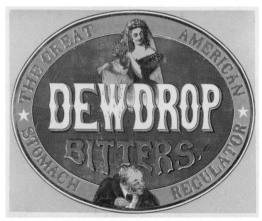

This Dewdrop Bitters magazine advertisement shows a woman, perhaps a goddess of nature, dripping dew into the glass of the man standing below her.

its power to soothe throats and intestines, was also a widely used ingredient.

More than a few of the mysterious liquids created in the cellars of medieval monasteries led to botanical libations that we still consume today, most typically, in the hour or two following a meal. The French label these comforting elixirs as *digestifs*. The Italians call them *digestivos*. Others who believe in their therapeutic powers refer to them as bitters.

Popular herbal liqueurs, most notably, Chartreuse and Benedictine D.O.M., both French in origin, were invented centuries ago. Other newer after-dinner libations, like Baileys Original Irish Cream and Carolans Finest Irish Cream, are popular, in part, because they are creamy, thick and low in alcohol (less than 20 percent alcohol by volume). Some believe that cream is desirable in proper digestion due primarily to the fact that it coats the esophagus and the stomach lining, lessening acidic irritation.

To this day, after-dinner liqueurs are viewed by millions of people the world over as one of the more civilized ways to bring down the curtain on the day and to ease a person's system into the restful evening. But, in reality, liqueurs are much more than "soothe operators;" they also are widely used in thousands of cocktail recipes.

Happy hour

During the mid-nineteenth century in thriving American cities like New Orleans, San Francisco, St. Louis, and New York, modern cocktails took shape through the creativity of visionary bartenders who saw past just serving beer, brandy, or whiskey to thirsty patrons. Using base spirits, most prominently, whiskey, gin, rum, and brandy, these pioneering mixologists experimented by employing vermouths and liqueurs—like orange bitters, absinthe (still legal in the United States in the 1800s and, happily, legal once again), Peychaud's or Angostura bitters, and fruit and flower liqueurs—as sweetening agents.

The bartenders did this to replace bland simple syrup as a sweetener to early cocktails like sours, punches, flips, and fizzes. The addition of a finely made liqueur heightened the flavor intensity of the cocktail and added new dimensions of taste that could never be achieved by the use of simple syrup.

By the gay nineties—the 1890s, that is—bartenders in metropolitan restaurant bars, saloons, and hotels were regularly adding liqueurs like curaçao, absinthe, and anisette to mixed drink recipes. Accordingly, the importation of liqueurs, produced mostly in Italy, France, and Germany, to America dramatically increased. Just prior to World War I, urban America was well accustomed to liqueurs primarily through the vehicle of the cocktail.

Following World War II, American consumer interest in cocktails and, therefore, liqueurs, advanced even more with the institution of the "happy hour." This national phenomenon was a two-hour buffer zone that eased the middle class from the eight-hour workday into the recreational pleasures of the evening. From the late 1940s into the early 1960s, liqueurs such as Irish Mist, Drambuie, Grand Marnier, Benedictine D.O.M., Cointreau, Di Saronno, Frangelico, and Galliano became staples in restaurants and bars across the United States.

From the mid-1960s to the mid-1970s, the character

The growing popularity of Baileys Original Irish Cream liqueur, pictured above on ice with a cinnamon stick, has led the company to introduce new flavors.

of liqueurs forever changed with the introductions of Kahlúa (1962) and Baileys Original Irish Cream (1974). These two less herbal-botanical, low-alcohol liqueurs— ergo, less medicinal tasting—started a revolution in liqueurs that continues to the present day. Suddenly, liqueurs appealing to female consumers began springing onto the marketplace, and the world of beverage alcohol was altered forever.

Nowadays, the liqueur sector is one of the fast-growing subcategories of the greater spirits category. As contemporary consumers become more open to spirits history and dare to dabble in the mysteries of cocktails, a major source of liqueur usage, liqueurs will continue to enchant and delight spirits sophisticates.

CHAPTER SIX

A Master Tasting Class: Appreciating Spirits

A taster in Scotland sniffs a sample of Bruichladdich's quadruple-distilled single-malt whisky from a *copita*.

The biggest challenge in becoming even a moderately astute taster of fine spirits isn't as much in mastering the art of proper tasting as much as in developing a mental archive of taste experiences. Feeding this archive data takes time. All top-notch tasters continually work at cultivating their tasting abilities as well as their recalling skills, remembering what they've sampled over the years. With distilled spirits being such a bottomless topic, no one ever reaches the end of the trail—and that's the fun of it.

Let's discuss some fundamentals.

Did you know that your sense of smell constitutes up to 90-percent of your sense of taste, is your most primitive sense, and is your primary sense in triggering memory? Therefore, the sense of smell, guided by an internal network of damp, spongy membranes located behind one's eyes is the pivotal sense when unearthing the innate virtues of single malts or, for that matter, anything with scent or flavor. Your olfactory sense, then, is the key that will unlock your personal treasury of genuine single-malt enjoyment.

The tip of the tongue detects sweetness; taste buds on the sides of the tongue pick up sourness; the tongue's rear section recognizes bitterness; and nearly the entire surface of the tongue, but particularly the front, identifies saltiness. Bitterness is the fundamental flavor to which we are all the most sensitive from birth and is likewise the one that takes the longest to like.

Umami, a Japanese discovery, is a relatively new taste concept to the West and is now widely considered the fifth primary taste. *Umami* is most appropriately depicted as an intensely savory, broth-like quality unrelated to the other four primary tastes. One experiences umami when you taste things such as dried mushrooms, shellfish, juicy steak, ripe tomatoes, or Parmesan cheese.

Tasting like a professional taster begins with these criteria:

• Understanding the five primary flavors and how they relate to the beverage category

• Creating a personal tasting format in which one's senses of smell and taste learn to work in coordination to mine the most information for your taste archives

• Learning how to recognize "thumbprint" experiences, meaning becoming adept at identifying individual spirits' distinctive characteristics that make them stand out from the pack

• Remembering your impressions to compile an experiential library.

Ultimately, it's the thumbprints that determine the breadth and depth of one's comprehension and, by extension, the degree of enjoyment over time. Most consumers can turn themselves into perceptive spirits tasters within two to three years if they are diligent. Five years, if they are more casual in their approach.

Spirits tasting 101:
The indispensable "hows"

• Always taste fine spirits with friends for the purpose of sharing impressions and, thereby, learning from each other. Your growth as a taster will expand significantly faster if you taste as part of a regular group. (Useful aside: this helps to keep costs down, as well!)

• If, say, you are sampling single-malt Scotches, start out by tasting at least four but no more than six whiskies just to become accustomed to the wide array of smells, tastes, and textures of spirits. As you get more experienced, begin to focus your "flights" more on individual whisky-making areas, like Islay, Speyside, and the Lowlands.

• Next, start to examine the various malt whisky expressions of individual distilleries. The key to steadfast learning is to continue to narrow your focus, so that pivotal differences of individual whiskies become glaringly apparent after you've established the ground floor of your mental archive.

• Taste blind. This means taste the spirits without knowing what they are in order to challenge your senses. By heightening your awareness in tasting the unknown, your senses of smell and taste sharpen tenfold. Trust your nose and your 10,000 taste buds. Blind tasting, of course, requires somebody to organize the tasting for the group.

• Never use plastic glasses or paper cups. Do not use squat double old-fashioned tumblers. The best glass by a wide margin for all types of brandies, whiskeys, liqueurs and white spirits is a 5- to 6-ounce, short-stemmed, tulip-shaped, tapered wine glass with a narrow rim, called a *copita*. The idea is to funnel the aroma into the nasal cavity to give the olfactory sense the best chance of forming clear impressions, impressions that will assist you in forming opinions about styles and types of single malts. Copitas are the traditional glass of Spanish Sherry producers and the most widely employed glass type in the whiskey and brandy industries. Quality spirits deserve quality glassware in order to showcase their virtues.

Quality glassware enhances the olfactory experience of spirit-tasting.

• Arrange the flight in order of lowest in "alcohol by volume", a.b.v., to highest in a.b.v. If all spirits chosen are the same abv, arrange from youngest to oldest.

• Pre-pour all the spirits in your test flight, two ounces of room temperature spirit at a time, and number them. Measure so that you get used to seeing what two ounces look like. You need enough liquid in order to smell it twice and taste it at least twice.

• Make certain to employ spittoons during blind tasting sessions; opaque 16-ounce plastic cups work well. Consumption of alcohol impairs anyone's ability to keenly taste, recognize, gather data, and learn. Save the imbibing for afterward.

• As a matter of routine, have plenty of mineral water, bland cheeses like mild cheddar, Muenster, Monterey jack, and neutral-tasting crackers close at hand to counter the alcohol as well as to cleanse the palate between tastes.

• Last, refrain from using anthropomorphic terms (muscular, handsome, feminine, masculine, sassy, laughing, timid, and the like) when describing spirits. They're dumb-sounding and don't enlighten to the topic matter. It's preferable to emulate the preeminent master distillers who instead relate what they smell and taste to commonplace items, such as fruits (tropical, red, yellow, dried) and nuts; spices and mint (peppermint, spearmint); citric, tannic acids; flowers; candies; baked goods like breads, cookies, pastries, yeast and dough; smoke, tobacco, ashes, soot; coffee, cocoa, tea; and, naturally, the basic four of sweet, sour, bitter, salty.

Evaluating the distinctions in single-malt Scotch whiskies

Learning how to evaluate finer spirits can be illuminating and entertaining. Using single-malt Scotch whiskies as an example, here's how one can break down a flight of whiskies in an orderly manner.

Presently, there are around 90 operating single-malt distilleries spread out over Scotland's islands and mainland. The paramount pleasures of single-malt appreciation accelerate when you begin to recognize regional and—the ultimate kick—individual distillery characteristics. Initially, put aside anything that you've read or heard about Scotland's so-called whisky districts. These loose definitions do not assist the average punter in becoming more astute in the early days.

Ignore the districts concept in favor of learning how first to determine whether or not a whisky comes from a malt distillery that's positioned near the sea—call those "maritime malts"— or from a distillery that's located in the Highlands away from the coast— "inland malts." By starting with these two basic situational facets, you'll gradually learn how to identify more specific locations.

Reduce the possibilities of a single malt's place of origin by using the deduction method, meaning, figure out what the single malt *is not* and work backwards from there. If the whisky's an inland single malt, it's highly unlikely that there will be evidence, faint or potent, in the aroma or taste of saltiness, sea air, seaweed, brine, or dill. Maritime malts, on the other hand, won't typically emit scents or flavors of cereal grain, flowers, minerals, or fruit *without* some indication of saltiness or brininess.

Many single malts from Scotland have a smoky quality from peat. Peat is vegetation that's halfway to becoming coal and is commonly employed in Scotland's whisky industry to dry dampened barley in kilns. The smokiness from peat can appear in either maritime or inland malts. Peat gives off smoky, ash-like qualities in single malts that vary in degree from light and sweet to heavy and medicinal. Amount of peatiness is not a quality factor, but more a stylistic aspect.

Younger single malts (15 years old and younger) will taste fresh, intensely grainy, and vibrant while older malts will feature stronger flavors than can seem woody, resiny, honey-like, or spicy. Age is not a determination of quality. In fact, many single-malt Scotches are at their peak in the 12- to 20-year range.

Finally, as you are savoring the single malts in your tasting, take note of the one characteristic of each that speaks the loudest to you and file that trait away in your private archive for future reference. It's usually that attribute that will be the all-important thumbprint. Each single-malt whisky, or any better spirit, for that matter, has a distinct benchmark virtue that has occurred because of how the whisky was distilled; or because of the type of oak barrel that it was stored in; or because of where the distillery sits; or perhaps due to the water that was used. Any number of environmental or production effects can form the thumbprint that will stick with you. It's these inherent peculiarities that will form the foundation of your spirit library, brick by brick by brick.

CHAPTER SEVEN

Spirits and Cocktails in the Home

Home bartenders need a variety of tools to learn the art of mixology.

The Home Bartending File

Every amateur bartender must begin with the basics, both with tools and mixed drink recipes. While this is not a cocktail book, it is absolutely necessary at this juncture to cite specific things that are required to make the spirits in one's home into savory cocktails. For much more extensive coverage on these topics, pick up these three foundational books on the art and skill of genuine mixology: Gary Regan's *The Joy of Mixology,* David Wondrich's *Killer Cocktails* and Dale DeGroff's *The Craft of the Cocktail.*

Following the accumulation of your spirits collection, here's what's needed on the mixology side.

The 12 must-have home bartending tools

- **Paring, chef's, and channel knives**
- **Wooden muddler**
- **Ice tongs**
- **Boston shaker** (metal base with pint glass top)
- **Stainless steel Cobbler shaker**
- **Julep and Hawthorn strainers**
- **Hand citrus juicer**
- **Long-handled cocktail spoon**
- **Wait staff corkscrew**
- **Bottle opener**
- **Microplane grater**

• **2 double-sided measuring jiggers** (1 and 2-ounce; ¾ and 1½-ounces)

The 12 foundational cocktails that every home bartender should know

Since the amounts of these basic ingredients vary from mixologist to mixologist, from cocktail recipe book to cocktail recipe book, exact amounts are not cited below. It is from these dozen cocktails that scores of cocktails are born. Know these twelve, and you'll be ahead of the crowd.

• **Classic Dry Martini** (London dry gin, vermouth)

• **Margarita** (Tequila, Cointreau, lime juice)

• **Bloody Mary** (vodka, lemon juice, Worcestershire sauce, Tabasco, tomato juice, salt, and pepper)

• **Daiquiri** (light rum, simple syrup, lime juice)

• **Manhattan** (straight rye whiskey, sweet vermouth, Angostura bitters)

• **Old-Fashioned** (straight Bourbon whiskey, Angostura bitters, orange slices, sugar, club soda, maraschino cherries)

• **Cosmopolitan** (citrus vodka, Cointreau, lime juice, cranberry juice)

A foundational knowledge of cocktail recipes allows mixologists to get creative in their craft.

- **Mojito** (light rum, lime juice, simple syrup, mint sprigs, club soda)

- **Pisco Sour** (pisco, lemon juice, simple syrup, egg white, Angostura bitters)

- **Caipirinha** (cachaça, simple syrup, lime)

- **Sidecar** (Cognac, Cointreau, lemon juice)

- **Irish Coffee** (Irish whiskey, coffee, unsweetened cream, brown sugar syrup)

The 10 Essential Home Bar Cocktail Glasses

An integral part of any cocktail's aura is how the mixologist presents the cocktail. To that successful end, having the right glassware is as paramount as having the right tools and the right spirits.

Here are the "absolutely necessary" ten:

- **Martini glass, or cocktail glass,** for all cocktails that are served "up"

- **Double old-fashioned glass, or a rocks glass,** for all spirits and cocktails served over ice

- **Highball glass** for highballs, beer, and soft drinks

- **Champagne flute** for Champagne and Champagne cocktails

- **All-purpose wine glass** for white, rosé, and red wines, as well as frozen cocktails

- **Shot glass** for all shooters

- **Port or Sherry glass—a copita,** for liqueurs, finer spirits served neat, dessert wines, and fortified wines

- **Pint or pilsner glass** for most beer and ale service

- **Collins glass, or a chimney glass,** for tall drinks

- **Toddy mug** for all seasonal warm or cool drinks, like toddies and punches

Spirits for the Home Bar

Anyone who entertains at home should have a well-stocked collection of fine brandies, whiskeys, white spirits, and liqueurs, as well as the necessary supplementary beverages that often accompany fine spirits in cocktail recipes. Purchasing is simple since most high-quality beverage alcohol retailers carry far more than merely the spirits essentials. Online sources usually offer more than adequate inventories, but in both cases it's always best to shop around since prices and services can vary widely.

A good home bar must have certain items for mixing purposes. Here are the absolute essentials for each level of the home bar:

Basic home bar:

- London dry gin
- Unflavored vodka; citrus-flavored vodka
- Angostura bitters
- Light rum
- 100-percent agave blanco Tequila
- VSOP Cognac
- Blended Scotch whisky; blended Irish whiskey
- Straight Bourbon whiskey; Tennessee sour mash whiskey
- Cream liqueurs; coffee liqueurs
- Fruit liqueurs (orange/Triple Sec)

Experienced drinker's home bar:

- London dry gin; Plymouth gin

- Unflavored vodka; flavored vodka; (citrus, orange, berry, coffee or chocolate)

- Angostura bitters; Peychaud's bitters

- Light rum; gold rum

- Cachaça

- 100-percent agave blanco and reposado Tequila

- VSOP and XO Cognac

- Pays d'Auge Calvados; applejack

- Peruvian or Chilean pisco

- Blended and single-malt Scotch whisky; blended Irish whiskey

- Straight Bourbon whiskey; Tennessee sour mash whiskey

- Dry and sweet vermouths

- Cream liqueurs; coffee liqueurs

- Fruit liqueurs (orange or Triple Sec); nut liqueurs; herbal liqueurs

- Bitter liqueurs (Campari, Fernet Branca)

Expert's home bar:

- London dry gin; Plymouth gin; Dutch Genever

- Unflavored vodka; flavored vodkas; (citrus, orange, berry, coffee, or chocolate)

- Angostura bitters; Peychaud's bitters; Regan's bitters

- Light rum; single-barrel rum; rhum agricole; dark rum

- Cachaça

- 100-percent agave blanco, reposado, anejo, and extra anejo Tequila

- VSOP and XO Cognac; vintage Armagnac

- Pays d'Auge Calvados; Domfrontais Calvados; applejack

- Peruvian pisco

- California or Oregon alembic brandy

- Blended and single-malt Scotch whisky; blended Irish whiskey

- Straight Bourbon whiskey; Tennessee sour mash whiskey

- Small-batch or single-barrel straight Bourbon whiskey

- Straight rye whiskey

- Dry and sweet vermouths

- Cream liqueurs; coffee liqueurs

- Fruit liqueurs (orange/Triple Sec); nut liqueurs; herbal liqueurs (Chartreuse, Benedictine)

- Apéritifs (Lillet, Pineau des Charentes)

- Bitter liqueurs (Campari, Fernet Branca)

Spirits storage and aging

Fine spirits should be treated with all the respect given to fine wine. In other words, keep spirits in the dark, cool, but not necessarily refrigerated, places. Like any perishable commodity, spirits breakdown chemically when stored for long periods in places that are excessively bright and hot. They become flabby and dull. They lose their acidity. Vodkas and gins can be kept refrigerated; brandies, whiskeys and oak-aged rums and Tequilas needn't be stored in mechanically chilled spaces but should be kept in cool closets, cabinets, or cellars.

Once distilled spirits are bottled, they cease changing. So there is no reason to store spirits as one some-times stores wine to improve or mellow with age. Red and some white wines often do; but spirits won't change. Once you buy a bottle of spirits, it's ready to be opened and enjoyed.

The lifespan of an open bottle of spirits

Unlike wines and beers that have scant shelf time once they are opened (a day, maybe two), opened spirits can last for months. Still, once air invades the bottle cavity, the chemical make-up of the liquid starts to change, and not for the better. Likewise, bear in mind that as the con-tent of the bottle dwindles over time due to usage, more air mingles with what's left in the bottle, diminishing the spirit's freshness even further.

Here's an approximate timeframe schedule for opened spirits, with the understanding that it's better to lean to the shorter end of the scale than the longer:

- **White Spirits: 2-3 months**
- **Whiskeys: 4-5 months**
- **Brandies: 3-4 months**
- **Liqueurs: 3-4 months** (cream liqueurs should be refrigerated after opening)

Serving white spirits

Gin and vodka generally are included as part of a mixed drink, but on occasion it is surprisingly nice, if not dar-ing, to serve them on their own, especially ice-cold fla-vored vodkas. Traditionally, Poles and Russians imbibe vodka on its own in small measures and usually with food. Use a small 2-ounce stemmed glass called a "cordial

A shooter of vodka

glass" for maximum impact and an elegant look to boot. Gin can be enjoyed well-chilled in a cocktail glass that's been rinsed with lime juice.

Tequila is the heart of the most popular cocktail in North America, the margarita, yet it is particularly bright when served chilled in a shot glass with a lime wedge. Try 100-percent agave reposado Tequila for this exercise; this class of Tequila possesses more than ample herbal agave scent and oaky smoothness to make it on its own. Mescal is served best unadulterated so that the deep vegetal, herbaceous quality of the agave can come through.

Serving whiskey

Aside from the myriad cocktail possibilities for whiskey, many of the better whiskeys are best when served unadulterated in either a 10-ounce double old-fashioned glass or a 6-ounce stemmed Spanish copita. These whiskeys include all single-malt Scotch whiskies; single-malt and pure pot still Irish whiskeys; small batch, single-barrel, older (10-plus years) straight Bourbon or Tennessee sour mash whiskeys; older (8-plus years) Canadian whiskies.

Whiskeys should always be served at room temperature along with a small pitcher of room temperature mineral water in case the drinker likes to dilute his whiskey. Water arouses any of whiskey's aromatic properties.

When ice cubes are required, never use ice made with tap water, which often contains chemicals like fluoride, chlorine, and lead. These types of chemicals destroy any finer whiskey's freshness, graininess, and core identity. It's far better to freeze mineral water into cubes.

Serving brandy

For centuries, it's been the custom to serve finer brandies in onion-shaped, short-stemmed, 10- to 14-ounce glasses called snifters. The original idea was to allow the brandy to warm up. This age-old concept has been shot down in light of brandy producers themselves asking consumers to move past snifters and instead begin employing small, stemmed, tulip-shaped copitas that hold no more than six ounces of liquid. The reason is simple: the smaller area focuses the aroma better and the shape funnels the fragrance upward, making the whole experience deeper and truer. The problem with snifters is that the natural, often subtle aromas of fine brandies dissipate too quickly in the large space of the snifter bowl.

Brandies should always be served at room temperature.

Serving Liqueurs

A recommended method of learning how to enjoy liqueurs is settling on when to serve them. After-dinner liqueurs are allowed to fulfill their promise when they are served after, not as an accompaniment to, the final course. Dessert or cheese courses should be paired with suitable libations, especially sweet or fortified wines. The whole idea of a *digestif* is to aid digestion, not be an integral part of it. Coffee or tea can absolutely be served alongside liqueurs.

Digestive liqueurs should provide a break, a respite in the festivities. Most professional party planners, caterers, restaurateurs, as well as seasoned private hosts recommend that after-dinner drinks be enjoyed away from the actual dinner table setting. Waiters in better eateries and clubs sometimes ask, "Would you care to have your coffee and liqueurs in the library in front of the fire?"

The reasons for decampment prior to the serving of after-dinner liqueurs are two-fold. One, by relocating, the party members can stretch their legs and actually stimulate digestion by the mere actions of standing and walking, even short distances. Sitting is the worst position for easy digestion.

Two, the introduction of new surroundings transports the party into a refreshed frame of mind. A change of scenery delicately suggests the conclusion to the serving of food and the ushering in of a round of different libations. In other words, the meal is finished, but the evening needn't be. Indeed, the evening can be extended and one's food can be settled with the imbibing of fine spirits and liqueurs.

Every spirits lover's personal responsibility

As always, moderation in alcohol consumption for everyone is strongly advised. In reality, the "moderate consumption" message means much more than just not imbibing to excess. It likewise means *never drinking alcoholic beverages of any type before operating heavy machinery.*

It means that anyone serving spirits should be watchful of his guests and when one appears to be overdoing it, that host has the responsibility to immediately stop serving. Being responsible means calling for a taxi when a guest looks even the slightest bit tipsy, or arranging for another guest to take them home.

A sound and reliable antidote to problematic drinking is to make certain that plenty of food and water are within everyone's reach right from the beginning of the event. In fact, one of the hottest trends is pairing food with spirits and cocktails. Food frequently brings out otherwise hidden pleasures in straight spirits or mixed drinks.

Being a socially responsible host means thinking much further beyond the circle of one's friends and guests. It means taking into account the welfare of one's neighborhood, one's section of town, and one's entire city and county. Serving spirits automatically means that steps must be taken to safeguard the welfare of everyone within your sphere of influence.

CHAPTER EIGHT

Glossary

Absinthe: A distillate originally based on grape eaux-de-vie and steeped or rectified with several herbal and botanical ingredients, including hyssop, lemon balm, anise, Chinese aniseed, fennel, coriander and other roots and herbs. An important, if controversial, ingredient, wormwood oil, was responsible for the nearly-worldwide ban on the production of absinthe, when it was determined that it contained thujon, a strong drug that causes epileptic-type seizures when taken in large quantities. There is scientific agreement today that absinthe's high proof of 130 percent was more problematic then the chemicals in the herbal ingredients in their tiny amounts, and it is no longer banned in the U.S.

Agave: A large plant indigenous to Mexico that looks like a cross between a giant pineapple and a cactus. The plant is actually a member of the lily family. There are roughly 400 varieties of agave, cultivated and wild. The Weber Blue Agave is used to make Tequila.

Aged (in oak): The process of storing wine and spirits in oak barrels for a period of time to remove harsh flavor notes and add specific characteristics found in the wood. The age, previous use, and size of the barrels used determine the oak effects.

The barrels are often charred inside to introduce additional flavors from the caramelized sugars in the oak.

Aguardiente: Literally translates to burning water, it is the word used in Spanish-speaking countries for brandy. (*Aguardente* in Portugal.)

Akvavit, Akavit, Aquavit: Grain-based spirit made in Scandinavian countries, flavored with different herbs, the most common of which are caraway and fennel. Translated "water of Life."

Alambic or alembic still: The original single-batch pot still, thought to have originated in India and Pakistan, perfected in the Middle East, and brought to Europe by the Islamic Moors. The first distilling of any kind in Europe probably took place in Sherisch, which was the Moorish name for the town of Jerez de la Frontera.

Alcohol, Ethyl: Beverage alcohol widely believed to be derived from the Arabic word *al koh'l*. Kohl is a fine powdered cosmetic used by Arabic women for eye shadow.

Amaretto: Almond- and apricot-flavored liqueur, originally made in Italy, but now made in other countries as well.

Amaro: Italian liqueurs made from grape eaux-de-vie and bitter herbs, usually served after a meal as a digestivo.

Añejo rum: rum aged in oak barrels; the aging requirements vary from nation to nation.

Angostura Bitters: J.G.B. Siegert, a young German army doctor who volunteered to fight for Simon Bolivar and Venezuelan independence from Spain, first created Angostura Bitters in 1824 as a stomach tonic for Bolivar's jungle-weary troops. His first production plant was in the town of Angostura in Venezuela. Today, made on the Island of Trinidad. The formula is secret, but the top flavor notes are cinnamon, allspice, and clove. Angostura is officially categorized as a food additive, even though it is 40 percent alcohol.

Anisette: A liqueur made in many countries that is flavored with aniseed; thought to be French in origin.

Aperitif: A drink before the main meal to stimulate the appetite, from the Latin word *aperire*, it means "to open." Can encompass anything from wine: flavored, aromatized and fortified wines; cocktails; and Champagne.

Applejack: Whiskey made from a mash of at least 51 percent apples that is fermented, then distilled. The Lairds company in New Jersey has been making applejack since colonial times, and thus is sometimes referred to as Jersey Lightning. Applejack is usually bottled at 40 percent alcohol.

Aqua vitae: Latin; means "water of life."

Arak, Arrack, Raki: A clear distillate originally made from date palm, now also made from rice and sugar cane. Arak was the base for the first punch drinks in the 17th century, a tradition brought home to England from India by the British tea and spice traders. Today, it is made in the Middle East, India, and Southeast Asia.

Armagnac: French grape brandy from the departemente of Gers in southwestern France. Single distilled in a special still, Armagnac is considered a stronger style than Cognac. There are three recognized brandy districts in Armagnac, Bas Armagnac (the best), Ténarèze, and Haut Armagnac.

Blended Scotch whisky, Scotch blended: A blend of pot still single-malt Scotch whiskies (malted barley) and column still grain (wheat, corn) whiskies. Ratio is typically 30-35 percent single-malt and 65-70 percent grain whiskey.

Blended straight whiskey: A blend of 100 percent straight whiskies of the same type, like rye, Bourbon, or corn from different distillers or from different seasons within one distillery.

Blended whiskey: A minimum of 20 percent straight whiskeys blended with neutral grain whiskey.

Bonded whiskey: Whiskey "bottled in bond" is stored in a government warehouse from between four and 20 years. It is not taxed until after it is bottled, a practice started in the 19th century to protect the whiskey maker from paying tax on spirits that evaporated during aging. Bonded whiskey is bottled at 100-proof (50 percent alcohol), under government supervision.

Bourbon: American whiskey made from a mash of at least 51-percent corn (a small amount of barley, then either rye or wheat fills out the rest of the mash) and aged for at least two years in charred oak barrels. Can be legally produced in any state. Cannot be distilled at higher than 160-proof (80 percent alcohol).

Brandy: From the Dutch term *brandewijn*, "burnt wine." Distilled spirit derived from fermented fruit.

Cachaça: A sugarcane spirit made in Brazil, usually distilled from fresh-cut cane and usually bottled without oak aging.

Calvados: An oak-aged brandy made from a mash of up to 48 different apple varieties and a small percentage of pears in the Normandy region of France, in the departemente of Calvados.

Cassis or Crème de Cassis: A liqueur made from blackcurrant berries that originated in Dijon, Burgundy, but is now made throughout France. Makes a drink called a Kir, a small amount of cassis in a glass of white table wine. The Kir Royale is the same drink made with Champagne instead of white wine.

Congeners: Impurities carried along with the molecules of alcohol vapor during distillation. They may derive from the base fruit or grain used in the original mash, or other organic matter encountered during the different stages of beverage alcohol production. The congeners are the elements that give a spirit its distinctive taste and aroma. The chemical bonds between the congeners and the alcohol vapor can be broken by repeated distillation at high temperatures.

Continuous, Column or Patent Still: The two-column, metal plate, continuously running still system that was invented in the late 1820s by Robert Stein and Aeneas Coffey.

Curacao: A liqueur first made by the Bols Distillery in Holland from small bitter curacao oranges; now made in many countries, it comes in white, orange, and blue—the color being the only difference.

Distillation: The process of separating parts of a liquid mixture through boiling, evaporation, cooling, and condensation. Distillation is used to produce concentrated beverage alcohol, called ethanol.

Eau-de-vie: French for "water of life," but more specifically, a type of brandy made from fermented mash of fruit; occasionally aged in oak barrels. *Eaux-de-vie* has evolved to be defined as a group of unaged digestif brandies made from stone fruits and other fruits like raspberries and strawberries.

Esters: Acid compounds resulting from distillation that give fruit-like aroma to spirits.

Ethyl Alcohol Beverage: Alcohol produced by the fermentation of a sugar solution.

Fermentation: A process that breaks down sugar molecules into carbon dioxide gas and ethyl alcohol. This change is accomplished by the yeast micro-organism, classified as a plant, that reproduces itself rapidly in a solution containing sugar.

Gin: Grain spirit flavored with botanicals, specifically genièvre or juniper, and other flavors, including coriander, lemon peel, fennel, cassia, anise, almond, ginger root, orange peel, and angelica.

Grappa: Grappa is made from the leftover skins, seeds, and stems, called pomace, after grapes are pressed for wine in Italy. Grappa is usually unaged.

Grenadine: Sweet red syrup used in alcoholic and non-alcoholic drinks. The original flavor base was pomegranate, but many brands use artificial flavor. The real deal is still being made by Angostura, among others.

Infusion: A steeping process like that of tea-making. In beer and whiskey-making, the grains and malted grains are soaked in hot water several times, often with increasingly higher temperatures, resulting in a sweet liquid called wort. Infusion is also used in the production of fruit liqueurs, where fruit and other flavors are steeped in brandy or neutral grain spirits for any extended time.

Irish whiskey: A triple-distilled whiskey from Ireland. Thought to be the first whiskey. Irish whiskey is a blend of pot-stilled malt whiskey, pot-stilled unmalted barley whiskey, and column-stilled grain whiskey. Irish whiskey has a completely different character from its neighbor Scotland's whisky, mostly because the malt is not kilned or toasted with peat, so there is no smoky quality in the flavor.

Maceration: The steeping of herbs, botanicals, or fruits in spirits of some kind for a period of time, after which the whole mixture may be distilled again. This process is used to flavor different types of spirits such as liqueurs.

Marc: Made from the skins and seeds left over from the pressing in winemaking in France, called pomace. Marc is then fermented and distilled into an unaged brandy similar to Italy's grappa.

Mescal: The general category of agave-based spirit, which includes Tequila. All Tequila is mescal, but mescal is not Tequila. Mescal is made primarily in Oaxaca, Mexico, from the espadin species of agave, and sometimes bottled with the infamous worm or gusano in the bottle. Mescal has a smoky quality from the slow baking of the agave piña in clay ovens over hot rocks.

Mixto: Mixto is a Tequila-style spirit that is at least 51-percent blue agave spirit, but also contains sugars from cane or other sources.

Ouzo: Greek anise-flavored liqueur.

Peychaud's Bitters: Antoine Peychaud, owner of an apothecary shop in New Orleans, created an all-purpose flavoring and health tonic in 1793 from herbs and Caribbean spices that is believed to have been the first commercial bitters in the Americas. He combined the bitters with Cognac, called Sazerac de Forge et Fil, and it came to be known as a Sazerac.

Rum: Made from molasses, sugar cane juice, or sugar cane syrup, it is considered the first spirit of the new world. First produced in Barbados and Jamaica, traditionally double-distilled. *Rhum Agricole* is made from sugar cane juice not molasses.

Rye: Whiskey aged for a legal minimum of 2 years, with at least 51-percent rye in the mash.

Sake: Japanese wine made from fermented rice.

Sambuca: Anise-based, licorice flavored Italian after-dinner liqueur often taken with coffee. Black Sambuca was recently introduced to the American market under the names Opal Nera and Della Notte.

Schnapps: A Scandinavian and German term for strong, colorless spirits. Also known as snaps, the spirits may be flavored or unflavored. Today schnapps is a popular category of low-end fruit and spice spirits.

Single-malt Scotch: A 100-percent malted barley-based spirit produced by a single distillery in a pot still in Scotland. Bottled straight or used as a blending agent in blended Scotch.

Tequila: Produced only in Mexico, Tequila is derived from the Agave Tequiliana Weber Blue, one of the 400 varieties of the agave plant, a member of the lily family. Tequila comes in two main forms: mixto and 100-percent pure agave. Mixto is at least 51-percent agave with other sugars added to the agave during fermentation, usually from cane. As the name indicates, 100-percent pure agave Tequila is made only from agave.

Triple sec: A liqueur made from the curacao oranges first in France but now produced in many countries. Triple sec is mostly a mixer and unlike Cointreau is almost never taken straight. Famous cocktail applications are the margarita and the Long Island iced tea.

Uisge beatha: Literally translated to "water of life," the old Gaelic word for whisky in the British Isles. Some believe the Celtic pronunciation led to the English word *whisky*.

Vermouth: Fortified and flavored wine made in sweet or dry styles, used in cocktails and as an apéritif. The word originated from the German word for the wormwood plant, *wermuth*.

Vodka: From *voda*, the Russian word for water, vodka is distilled from grain and sometimes potatoes.

VS, VSOP, XO Cognac: Very Special; Very Superior Old and Pale; and Extra Old are designations used in Cognac and Armagnac to indicate minimum aging for their brandies. The actual age for the three designations vary from maker to maker.

Whiskey: From the Gaelic word, *uisge beatha*, meaning "water of life," whiskey is made from grain that is ground into grist, then cooked with water to release starches. Malt is added to convert the starch into sugar, and then yeast to begin the fermentation process. The low-proof liquid after fermentation is called beer, which after distilling, becomes whiskey.

Photography Credits